MT. DIABLO's commanding presence produces feelings of awe among many Walnut Creek, California, area residents and visitors. This panoramic view by photographer George Barber is from a spot across the road from Northgate High School, a short distance from the Old Borges Ranch.

Echoes from an Open Space Ranch

By Marnie White

Drawings by André Fairon
Photographs by George Barber
and Brian Murphy

Proceeds benefit
Walnut Creek Open Space and
Old Borges Ranch

Pleasant Hill Press, Lafayette, California

Published by
Pleasant Hill Press
473 Peacock Blvd.
Lafayette, CA 94549-5427

Library of Congress Cataloging-in-Publication

White, Marnie 1946-
Echoes from an Open Space Ranch / by Marnie White; drawings by
André Fairon; photographs by George Barber and Brian Murphy
ISBN 0-9649776-7-2
 1. White, Marnie, 1946- 2. Ranch life—California—Walnut Creek
Region. 3. Women ranchers—California—Walnut Creek Region—
Biography. 4. Ranchers—California—Walnut Creek Region—
Biography. 5. Walnut Creek Region (Calif.)—Biography.
6. Walnut Creek Region (Calif.)—Social life and customs. I. Title.

F869.W23 W47 2000
979.4'63—dc21   00-028341

9 8 7 6 5 4 3 2

Printed in the United States by
Morris Publishing
3212 East Highway 30
Kearney, NE 68847
1-800-650-7888

Contents

Acknowledgments

This book is dedicated to the memory of Bob Pond, Walnut Creek's first open space specialist.

I would also like to thank my dear husband Ranger Ron White, Daniel Borges, my two daughters Kristin and Kimberly, André Fairon, George Barber, Brian Murphy, Ted Fuller and his wife Norma Lent for their support and encouragement.

"Great Eagle, help me remember
that from above all things seem smaller.
Remind me to lift my great wings,
and fly above what may seem like boulders
before me here on the ground.
For when I spread my wings and rise above,
boulders are but tiny pebbles."
—Anon.

Illustrator André Fairon lives in Arcata, Calif., with his Siberian Husky, Shasta. He graduated in 1993 from the University of California at Santa Barbara with a B.A. in Film Studies and a minor in Animation. While there, he drew the "Andy Pharo" daily comic strip for the campus newspaper. In addition, he has illustrated newspaper editorials, various single-panel cartoons for magazines, a children's picture book entiitled "The Three Fishermen," sidewalk murals, portraits and several comic books in collaboration with other artists. In 1997, André held his first one-man art show. A talented artist in various media, he describes himself as mainly a comic book artist.

Photographer George Barber and his wife Dorothy and their son Steven, formerly from southern England, took up residency in California in 1980, and have never been tempted to leave. With a long career as a professional engineer, he traveled the world, visiting remote locations. His travel experiences inspired his love of photography, and his flair for life's natural beauty and simplicity clearly shows in his work.

Photographer Brian Murphy spent his childhood in and around the creeks and ponds in Walnut Creek where he developed a rapport with local wildlife. Exhibits of his photographs include a show at The Zahn Group in San Francisco. When he isn't working as a City of Walnut Creek engineering technician, he enjoys photographing wildlife in Walnut Creek Open Space areas and volunteering at the Lindsay Wildlife Museum, also located in the city. He says his picture-taking talent comes naturally, as he has not taken any formal instruction.

Introduction

"What the devil!" I yelled, as I stubbed my toe on another cast-off obstacle from someone else's past. Large raindrops plopped in the dust at our feet as my two daughters, eight-year-old Kristin and Kimberly, age one, and I scurried to the shelter of a dilapidated barn.

"Listen, Mommy. The mountain's tummy is growling," Kristin whispered. Another clap of thunder rumbled across the California hills. Then a bold streak of lightning illuminated the rickety skeleton of an old windmill.

"Whose?" I hollered over the din of thunder and rusty antique farm equipment creaking and clanking in the wind.

"You know, Mommy, the devil that lives up on the mountain, he's talking to us. My teacher told us about him. A long time ago, when he was a ghost, he scared some bad white people that made the Indians afraid of him."

"Humph, a devil indeed." But in a way, I believed her cock-and-bull story. Maybe some magic permeated the old Portuguese cattle ranch that was located right at the base of Mt. Diablo on the outskirts of Walnut Creek, California.

Early settlers named the mountain, and the Indians feared going there. For nearly a hundred and fifty years the hillsides lay in a natural state with the exception of a few scattered rural cattle ranches. Then in the early 1970s several of the ranchers who were losing money in the cattle business began selling parcels of their land to developers who envisioned housing tracts covering the hills. This created quite a stir among several concerned citizens in Walnut Creek. In 1974, these same citizens overturned a referendum and stopped development of their precious hills.

Contra Costa County voters passed a bond measure of $6.75 million for the purchase of more than 2,500 acres of prime oak woodlands and grassland savannah in the foothills of Mt. Diablo. Included in the purchase was the historic Old Borges Ranch dating back to the turn of the century.

Today, the ranch is completely restored with original cow and horse barns, first generation ranch house, wagon shed, woodshed, blacksmith shop, milk house, windmill, two-holer outhouse, corrals, cattle chutes and old-time farm equipment. The ranch is also home for numerous 4-H animals such as cattle, sheep, a horse, rabbits, pigs, chickens and goats. Below the ranch are the Hanna Grove Picnic Area, fishing pond, amphitheater and play area.

In 1981, the Borges Ranch and ranger station for the greater 1,400-acre Shell Ridge Recreation Area was placed on the National Register of Historic Sites and has since been proud to open its doors daily to the public and schoolchildren as a living part of our western heritage.

In time, my husband, Ranger Ron White, who was hired in 1978 as Walnut Creek's first open space ranger, many helping hands and I, would bring order to the past by restoring the old ranch house and barns, creating a living history program and helping develop a network of trails and recreational areas that encompass nearly 3,000 acres of open space for future generations.

After twenty-two years, I still sit in awe of the "Devil Mountain" listening to it growl while enjoying the cacophonous squawks and screeches from the barnyard.

He's Got to Be Kidding

The narrow dirt road was only wide enough for a single car and littered with potholes. "Ouch," I said, as I bumped my head on the roof of the jeep for the second time. I prayed we wouldn't meet another car coming in the opposite direction. My fears were soon calmed by the sound of rushing winter run-off tumbling over time-worn sandstone rocks in a wooded ravine to my left. The small stream followed the road for a short distance, then meandered through thick oak woodlands and bright green buckeye. In front of us a covey of California quail, their top-knots bobbing, hurriedly tiptoed across the road. A hawk fanned its red tail feathers and circled lazily above a field of brilliant yellow mustard. With a burr of the jeep's wheels over the cattle guard we arrived at an old cattle ranch. In front of us loomed a shack that looked like it had been blackened by a fire. At its hollow dark windows shreds of dirty white curtains flapped in the wind like flirting eyelashes beckoning us to venture further.

We passed two large barns, one nearly toppled on its side, the other barely standing, and rolled to a stop in front of a small ramshackle farmhouse.

The open space specialist, Bob Pond, turned to us and smiled. "Welcome to your new home, folks." My husband Ron and I both stared in disbelief and whispered to each other, "He's got to be kidding."

As we stepped out of the jeep, a loud ominous bellowing sound welcomed us. Directly across the road in front of the house was a corral. In the corral a large red bull with horns again roared powerfully. The bull's nostrils flared as he spewed up the dirt with his front hooves, eyeing our every move.

Bob Pond said that before the ranch was sold to the Walnut Creek Open Space in 1976, it had been a thriving cattle ranch, dating back to the turn of the century, but over the years had fallen into disrepair. The rancher who owned the bull now leased the grazing rights and the use of the barn from the open space. Bob assured us that the bull was gentle, but Ron, our eight-year-old daughter Kristin, one-year-old daughter Kim and I, having never been around a bull before, weren't quite that convinced.

We turned our backs on the "friendly" beast, and the open space specialist escorted us around the house. Cautiously we tramped through a yard cluttered with sections of a bygone picket fence, rusty cans, barbed wire, piles of rotting boards, tarred roofing paper, smelly garbage, discarded lawn chairs, and old plumbing fixtures. The house showed faint traces of having been painted white long ago, and its roof was peppered with holes where the shakes had blown off. Several windows were missing, and bricks from the chimney were strewn about the yard.

A couple of kids wearing stocking caps, down jackets and rain boots ran to greet us, and a man on a ladder waved. "We hired that fellow and his wife to renovate the old house and make it livable for the new ranger," Bob said. We just smiled and waved back.

A nauseating smell of fresh cow manure drifting from the barnyard made our noses twitch. A creepy feeling came over me, as I suddenly noticed a battalion of half-starved cats eyeing us from every direction. As we rounded a corner of the house, a gray long-haired Persian brushed its matted fur up against the back of my leg, sending prickles up my spine. I stood there in a dazed stupor. Did I hear the man right? Did they really expect us to live in this old derelict of a house?

The presence of someone tugging on my arm and the faraway cry of a child screaming, "Mommy! Come on!" jarred my senses. Being careful not to trip over more pickets and boxes of discarded junk, we made our way around the house and were soon intrigued by an unusual foundation made of concrete blocks embedded with oyster shells, horseshoes, old horse bits, a light bulb, measuring spoons, a toy gun, a kerosene lantern, various birth dates, and sayings such as "Welcome" and "Going My Way," which was the title of a

1940s movie starring Bing Crosby. There was even a pressed-glass chicken with real eggs inside it. Bob asked us what we thought of the wall. As experienced naturalists, our thoughts raced to school children tracing their curious fingers over the blocks. Ron and I looked at each other and without hesitating gave the same answer: It was terrific! Bob smiled, and we knew we had the job.

"What color of paint would you like on the house?" he asked. Ron and I agreed on a light tan with dark brown trim. Our tastes are similar. Then it was our turn: "Could we have horses, a dog, chickens and plant fruit trees?" To all of our questions, we got a firm "Yes."

On the way home in the car, Ron, Kristin and I talked over the pros and cons of the job. We wouldn't be in transit any more, expecting to move every six months to a year, as we did with the National Park Service. Ron would be doing what he liked to do best, managing almost 2,600 acres. We could have a garden, chickens and maybe a horse. But, oh, that house and the work ahead to get the ranch in shape. Did we have the foresight, and what it took to take on such a challenge, for Ron to become Walnut Creek's first open space ranger?

"Yes!"

The Move

The next day, Ron called up the open space specialist to tell him that he would accept the position. After he'd worked his last two weeks, we loaded up "Big Red," our trusty 1965 Ford pickup, which had taken us across the country so many other times with our meager furnishings, and headed for a new home.

The house had been painted, all right, but a watered-down white with pea-green trim— someone's interpretation of what a ranger's house should look like. A new asbestos roof had been put on the house, new fixtures in the closet-size bathroom, the kitchen and mud room painted a light cream color, and a chocolate brown carpet laid that wasn't supposed to show the dirt.

The county water district inspector arrived the next day, tested the water for drinking and informed us, after we had previously drunk pitchers full of the stuff, that it wouldn't kill us. But it would be advisable for us to bring in all of our drinking water until we could get a new well dug, since the old pinhole-ridden water pipes ran directly across the corral and had been snugly kept warm under a three-foot blanket of cow manure for the past forty years.

Not drinking the water, we assumed that we would have plenty of water for washing, bathing and irrigating. Unfortunately, Ron found out the hard way that washing and bathing couldn't be done on the same day.

Eager to get the kinks out from his first few days on the job, Ron stood in the tub, anxiously waiting for a flood of soothing warm bath water to drench his aching body. A gurgle emitted from the drain and a trickle of lukewarm water dripped slowly from the shower head. There was a deafening silence from the bathroom; then a rakish voice shouted, "Marn, I thought you told me that inspector said we had plenty of water. I can pee faster than what's coming out of here!"

Our first few weeks at the ranch were definitely not dull. The only heat in the house came from a large wood-burning cook stove in the kitchen and a dinky fireplace in the living room with half of its bricks missing. Ron was experienced with an axe and chopped and split wood after work to keep us warm. It was my job to stack it and bring in several armloads each day.

We stored boxes of books and various not-so-immediately-needed materials on the enclosed outside porch, called the mud room, until Ron could get some bookshelves made and a temporary office set up. The porch worked great as a storage room until the first night it rained, when we had to quickly rescue Ron's papers of ten years. Within a week we had a new roof on the porch, and I had proudly laid yellow and brown patterned tiles on the mud room floor and kitchen. Ron's folks and my dad came over to help, and between rain showers we dug post holes to replace a crumbling lichen-encrusted grape trellis and gathered all the pickets we could find to make a new used picket fence around the yard. This was how we discovered where the septic tank was located. Fifth hole going south on the back fence line we struck "pay dirt." A pungent odor of rotten eggs permeated the air for the next week. A plug of concrete was quickly made for the septic tank and a fence post placed gently over the spot with two feet cut off the top to match the level of the other posts.

20

SPINELESS prickly pear cactus, first introduced by Luther Burbank about 1900, was grown by Mary Borges. The world famous botanist believed a cactus like this, grown in the world's wastelands, could solve hunger problems for all, but he never succeeded in breeding a type without needles.

Meeting Dan Borges

Kristin, our oldest daughter, had started school and Ron was busy most of the time learning the ropes of the new job, so Kim, our one-year-old, and I were left alone at the ranch. From the kitchen window I looked out at a depressing scene of two old lawn chairs, an old rusty bathtub, and a pile of garbage and junk as high as our roof. Ranger Ron, my dear thoughtful husband, had a fourteen-foot garbage bin delivered to the ranch, which he said I could fill in my spare time.

So, after a day of thinking about it, I finally donned my blue jeans, an old parka and garden gloves, dragged the playpen out into the yard where Baby Kim could safely watch me, and went to work trying to melt down some of the trash. After two days of picking, I had barely made a dent. I was getting somewhat discouraged, to say the least, but vowed to discipline myself not to give up if it took me to the following year. But on the third day, a rider tied his horse up at the ranch. He sauntered over to where I was working and said, "I'm Dan Borges," as if his name was supposed to mean something to me. I then remembered Ron telling me that the Borges family had owned the ranch before the Walnut Creek Open Space bought it.

I introduced myself and continued going on about my business. I didn't know how he'd react to a couple of greenhorns coming in and taking over the ranch that his family ran for four generations. Besides, who was I to say anything? I was "only the ranger's wife."

ASTRIDE his horse Tuffy, Dan Borges makes a fine specimen of a cowboy.

I watched this cowboy put away his horse while I continued picking up more junk. He looked at me and I smiled at him. I guess he took it as an invite because he soon meandered over to the mound of trash, picked up the old bathtub that must have weighed nearly two hundred pounds, and tossed it into the bin as if it were foam rubber.

I wasn't going to argue with the man, so I cheerfully joined forces. For the next hour we worked together in silence, throwing box after box into the bin. As I worked, I studied this fine specimen of a cowboy. He was in his early fifties, stocky, with burly shoulders and muscular arms; his hair slightly salt and pepper. His suntanned face had a gentleness about it, and one eye was slightly cocked. I hoped he didn't notice me staring at him, but I really couldn't help myself. This was the closest I had ever been to a real cowboy. The only cowboys I had ever seen were John Wayne, Henry Fonda, and Slim Pickens in the movies or on television.

At the end of the hour he said, "It's time I headed home, but I'll be back tomorrow and give you a hand." I thanked him and waved an appreciative good-bye. After he left, I looked around and couldn't believe it; together we had picked up more junk in an hour than I had in the past three days. It made me feel somewhat useless. Dan came back the next day and the following. By the end of the week we had cleared out most of the garbage, and Ron and I had found a true friend.

Over the next ten years Dan Borges taught Ron and me many things about ranching. He showed us how to fix barbed wire fences, to make gates, round up cattle, brand and slaughter livestock, feed and care for farm animals, plus providing us with needed information about dams, wells, and the culture and lifestyle on a working cattle ranch.

George Barber

75TH BIRTHDAY party of Dan Borges on March 18, 2000, brings together, left, Robert Borges, the youngest son of Dan Borges, second from left. Next to him is his wife Barbara and their son, Dan Borges, Jr.

Compassion

I couldn't believe the knowledge and compassion Dan Borges possessed when it came to taking care of livestock. A few months after we came to the ranch a couple offered us the use of their Appaloosa horses in exchange for boarding, with the option to buy one of them. Eventually we bought Honey Bear, a sorrel mare with a frosted white blanket. Her hyperactive mate was a black and white Appaloosa stallion, loco enough to badly cut his right front leg on some barbed wire while trying to jump over the fence. The animal was in great pain and was hard to handle, so I asked Dan to help me. With his soft-spoken manner, Dan soon had the horse under control and tied up in a stall in the barn. Together we bathed the wound with warm water and Epsom salts. The horse continually kicked and whinnied from the sting, and wanted to bite us, as we slapped the salt solution on the cuts with a wet rag tied to the end of a broomstick. After our treatment, that horse never was very fond of either Dan or me, but we saved a fairly good horse.

Another time, an old cow after giving birth had a prolapse, in which the uterus became extended and came out. It looked like a giant red rose in full bloom. I felt so bad for that poor cow that it made my own backside smart. Ron, Dan, another rancher, and I managed to get the cow into the squeezer, a contraption that sandwiches the animal and confines it so that the rancher can work on it. Dan then proceeded to cleanse the area with antiseptic solution, and to neatly sew the cow's innards back inside her. At the first prick of the needle, "Old Bossy" bellowed so loud I had to hold my hands over my ears, but I soon learned certain procedures that may seem cruel are sometimes necessary to save an animal's life.

Another time, a cow aborted her calf and became bogged down in a mud hole. She later developed pneumonia and was in real bad shape when Dan found her. Most men would have put the cow down, but not Dan. He dragged her back to the ranch on a pallet and laid her in the barn on some fresh straw. Then he went to work rigging up a sling with a block and tackle to hoist the cow up so that she would be on her feet and the pneumonia wouldn't get worse. Being stuck in the mud for such a long time, the cow had lost circulation in her front legs and could no longer stand on her own. Dan stayed with her all night, rubbing her legs to bring back the circulation and feeding her a mash of warm molasses and grain to keep her strength up. He talked and sang softly to her, encouraging her not to give up.

I came into the barn the next morning to help rub her legs. As we were rubbing her down, she rolled her big brown eyes at us with a look of thank you, and to tell us that she now had the will to recover. I knew from then on that farm animals would play a major role in my life.

George Barber

EARLY in the year 2000, the wagon shed, windmill and milk house looked like this.

Two White Leghorns and a Couple of Rhode Island Reds

One Saturday I got this brilliant idea to raise chickens. I didn't know the first thing about them. I was so ignorant, I didn't even know hens didn't need a rooster to lay eggs.

Enthusiastic to start my project, I visited the local library. After thumbing through several books on raising small livestock, I found two; each one included a chapter about chickens. One had colored prints of the different breeds. I studied the pictures and decided the White California Leghorns and a couple of fat Rhode Island Reds looked good. These books excelled in showing the different breeds, but neither one went into great detail on the actual care of these animals.

Not letting this discourage me, I figured through trial and error I would learn anyway. At the local feed and grain store I asked the clerk for two big Leghorns and a couple of Rhode Island Reds.

The young man chuckled at my ignorance and said, "Lady, all we carry are chicks."

I said, "Well, then, I'd like to see your Leghorn and Rhode Island Red chicks."

Shaking his head, he motioned me to the back of the store where he pulled back a curtain exposing a sea of peeping yellow fluff. The sign read, "Rhode Island Red Chicks 34 Cents Each."

What a bargain, I thought. I asked the clerk to box up five females and one male. He gave me a queer look, then randomly picked out six chicks and put them in the box.

"Now," he said, "I suppose you'll be needin' some chick mash, a feeder, water tray and some lime powder for white-washin' to keep down the chicken lice."

"What?" I said. "Is all that stuff necessary?"

I decided to take the chick mash, water tray and lime powder. An old shallow dishpan would do just fine for a feeder. With all the various sundries, the bill came to $27.52. My husband Ron was going to kill me.

I pulled my little Volkswagen Rabbit around in front of the loading dock, and an older fellow with a curved back put the chicks and their paraphernalia next to our daughter Kristin in the back seat.

By the time we reached home, Kristin had given all the chicks names: Peeper, Old Yeller, Spot, Dopey, Jinx, and Henry. "Don't get attached," I told her. "They're not pets." Luckily, Ron wasn't home when we arrived, so I welcomed a reprieve from hearing how much I had spent on my little project.

Kristin helped me put the chicks in an old rabbit cage on top of the clothes dryer, where the heat kept them warm underneath. We put Ron's gooseneck desk lamp over the top of the cage with the bulb positioned so that it would shine down on the chicks. Out of our own ingenuity, Kristin and I created a pretty good chick incubator. We filled the water tray and put the chick mash in a large mayonnaise jar lid, so that the chicks could reach it. Each morning Kristin helped me give the chicks their mash and fresh water and change the newspaper in the bottom of the cage.

All the chicks survived quite well, and within a few weeks were bloodying their heads on the top of the cage by trying to get out.

Ron's busy schedule prevented him from helping, so Kristin and I, using a bucket of assorted nails, hammer, baling wire and a scrap of chicken wire that I found in the back woodpile, took on the challenge of fixing up the old chicken coop. I first hammered down loose boards, then patched the holes by attaching pieces of chicken wire over them with baling wire. In the bare places, we nailed the remaining chicken wire.

After several hours, our knuckles scraped and raw, we stood back and looked at our unprofessional handiwork. The coop sagged a little to the left and looked like a shack out of the comic strip "Li'l Abner," but it would do just fine for our chicks until I could coax Ranger Ron into building a new one.

Next, I cleaned out the old chicken manure inside the coop. For two days I wore a kerchief tied snugly over my nose while I shoveled bag after bag of dry, dusty, white chunks. Dan told me that it wasn't "hot" any more and that I should spread it on the garden because it made great fertilizer.

After sweeping out the place, I mixed two cups of lime powder with five gallons of water. In the pail, it looked like watered-down skim milk. Kristin helped me paint every board and roost in the house. When we finished we were speckled with tiny white spots all over us, but the stuff washed off easily in the shower. When the white-wash was thoroughly dry, it turned the boards a chalky white. I was amazed at the difference. We put fresh straw on the floor and in the egg laying boxes. For an old coop, we thought the place looked quite comfortable and homey.

"Mommy, can we put the chicks in it now?"

"Yes, honey."

I carefully carried the rabbit cage out. We put

the cage on the floor and opened the cage door for the chicks to wander out, but they wouldn't budge. I had to grab them and force each one out. The brood scurried to a corner of the shed and huddled together. "What's wrong with them, Mommy? Don't they like their new home?"

"Kristin, I think they're scared. After living in a cage for a month, this place must be pretty big to them. Why don't we leave them alone for a bit, and maybe they won't be so frightened."

We put the chicks' water tray and the old dishpan full of mash on the floor in the corner and hoped they would find them. Then we closed the door.

The next morning we checked on the chicks and found them scattered about the coop. One was balancing on the roost and the rest were pecking at the mash and drinking the water. I'd hoped we'd find in the egg boxes four lovely laid eggs, but the boxes were empty.

Another month went by, and I was about ready to take the chickens back to the feed store and ask for my money back. Dan said, by putting some wooden eggs or golf balls in the boxes, I'd encourage the hens to lay. But even this didn't work. Then one morning I heard a faint "cock-a-doodle-doo" coming from the chicken house, then another crow, and another.

"Oh, no! We didn't have five roosters, did we?" I quickly dressed and ran out to the chicken shed. On the edge of the roost, the Rhode Island Red rooster stood tall, balanced, his rubbery red comb translucent with morning light, and iridescent green tail feathers fluttering. He flapped his wings several times and crowed loudly, "cock-a-doodle-doo."

A white Leghorn sat in one of the boxes and, in another, a Rhode Island Red hen. I gently felt underneath the Rhode Island Red and to my delight, discovered my first egg, a light brown oval that felt warm and soothing in my hand.

"Good chicken," I said, patting it on the head. It squawked and tried to peck me, but I didn't care. I was ecstatic. My chickens were now egg layers. I snatched the two eggs and ran with them to the house.

"Ron! Girls! Come quick! Look what I've got!" I showed them the two eggs. Ron smiled, chuckled and said, "I'll have mine sunny side up, please."

Traditional Cattle Roundup

One Saturday morning in April, I woke to the sounds of the dogs barking, horses whinnying, and the jangle of horse trailers pulling into the ranch at 5:30 a.m. for the annual spring cattle roundup. A half-dozen cowhands emerged from their pickup trucks and started unloading their horses and talking in muffled voices. Suddenly, Dan's voice stood out from the rest as he yelled, "Come on, boys. Let's go. It's gettin' late."

I watched them through the kitchen window give a final check of their cinches, take last-minute swigs of coffee from their thermos bottles, grind out cigarettes with their heels, and swing onto their mounts. With their horses puffing clouds of steam from the morning cold, the riders headed over the rise.

A couple of hours later, a cloud of brown dust and several piercing cowboy whoops announced their return. Our two daughters, some of the neighbors, and I hurried toward the corral fence for a front row seat.

Seeing 250 head of cattle charging down the trail at once with only a handful of cowboys flanked on either side, hollering and waving their hats in the air, was a very impressive sight, and somewhat frightening.

They swiftly herded the cattle down into the main corral, where a cowboy in his late fifties gingerly perched on the top of a fence post, counting off the cows, steers and calves as they went through the gate. Inside the corral, a few of the cowpunchers started cutting out the calves. A cacophony of cowboy whoops, obscenities, cows mooing, horses' hooves, the crack of a bull whip, tack jingling, horses snorting, and the slam-bang of the squeezer being shut was deafening.

They wore long-sleeved western shirts that clung to their bodies with dark sweat rings under their arms and on their backs and chests. A film of dirt stuck to their bloodstained blue jeans and their leather chaps, worn smooth in spots from constant rubbing against their saddles and tack. I stared at their dung-caked pointed boots stirring up brown powdery dust devils. Pushed down on their heads to shade their eyes, they wore soiled felt or straw broad-brimmed cowboy hats stained around the bands with sweaty salt rings, dirt and rust-colored squirts of dried blood from dehorning the calves. Over their noses they wore red or blue kerchiefs as filters. A thick blanket of fine dust and grit sifted down their shirts. This same grit made their skins crawl, teeth grate, dulled their hair and shrouded the noonday sun, making it appear as a large cream-colored disk pasted on a flat blue sky.

One of the cowboys started a fire. It heated the old hand-forged branding iron for the small calves. Several others herded the cattle into the chutes. They coaxed the cattle one by one through the chutes towards the squeezer, a giant green monster with the words POWDER RIVER inscribed across it. With a solid slam, two strong men clanked the levers shut, trapping the steer inside the squeezer's barred jaws. They then began working on the beast.

First an inspector checked the animal for noticeable diseases and maims, such as pink eye, wood tongue, black leg, pneumonia, cattle fever, hoof rot, sores, cuts, and parasites.

For pink eye and open wounds, the cowboys sprayed a circle of deep gentian violet "Wound-Kote" around the eye or on the infected area. To rid a steer of parasitic worms, they forced a pill down its throat with a long plunger. If a calf looked poorly, it received an immunization shot, called "Eight-Way."

If needed, the animal was then branded. A section just large enough for the brand on the rump or shoulder was shaved with an electric razor.

An experienced brander wielded a modern-day electric branding iron, looking like the coiled burner on an electric stove, or a calf iron to the rump or shoulder just long enough to singe the hair and sear the first few layers of skin without leaving a blur. The acrid smell of singed hair and burnt rawhide permeated the air and left a nasty taste in our throats.

Quickly the fellows painted grease on the fresh brand so the air wouldn't get to it and cause a burning pain. State law says cattle cannot be sold or slaughtered without a brand for identification. Dan also earmarked his cattle like his father and grandfather by slashing a section out of the ear with his knife, or piercing it with an identification tag like an earring.

The levers clanked again, letting the large steer out of the squeezer, wild-eyed with rage. Adding insult to injury, a blast of disinfectant spewed forth, ridding him of pesky lice and bott fly eggs.

Meanwhile at the smaller chute, some of the cowboys dehorned and castrated young bull calves. Dan, quick with the dehorner, usually only required one sharp precision cut to remove the horn nibs. He then quickly cauterized the wounds so the animal hardly bled. He was also superstitious and believed in the old wives' tale—the wounds wouldn't bleed as much if the animals were castrated and dehorned during the wane of the moon.

The roundup and branding lasted until about one in the afternoon. By then, everyone was hot, dusty, dry throated, dragging their boots and starving. Ten minutes later, a survival team made up of Dan's wife Barbara and several other ladies came to their aid with a scrumptious banquet-size meal.

Barbara, a terrific cook, brought sliced ham, fried chicken, baked beans, three kinds of salad—green, pasta and vegetable—homemade "hot" Jalapeño peppers, black olives, chocolate cake, ice cold beer and homemade wine called "Port-a-gee Pink."

Then someone would pull out a guitar or a harmonica, or the cowboys exchanged tall tales. This was my favorite part of the traditional cattle roundup at the Borges Ranch.

Large Enough for a Bear

One Saturday afternoon in the fall, while I was shoveling up horse manure in front of the barn, a lady with dark short hair and curious eyes came running up to me. In the corral, Honey Bear sloshed through brackish pools of rust-colored rain water to the corral fence, greeting the visitor. The lady looked at the horse.

"You live here?" she asked timidly, looking as though she might be trespassing, or doing something wrong by asking me.

"Yes, I'm the ranger's wife. We live in that house over there."

She looked in the direction of our ramshackle house.

"Oh. I'm a school teacher at Indian Valley School off Marshall Drive, near the open space. On weekends I like to hike past your ranch, because it reminds me so much of the farm I grew up on. I was wondering, do you think I could bring my fourth grade class here for a visit? They'd love it." Her eyes lighted up as she spoke.

I wasn't sure what to say, as I really didn't have any authority. I looked around at several scraps of rusty loose baling wire, a pile of boards with sharp nails sticking out of them, and the mound of putrefying horse manure at my feet.

"You want to bring your students here? The place is a mess. What if a kid gets hurt? It really isn't open to the public. I don't know when. . ."

"Oh, please," she said. "The school has insurance, and every kid has had a tetanus shot. Besides, it wouldn't be a real ranch without some junk lying around. I'd really like for my kids to see your ranch. Maybe they could help you feed the farm animals." I smiled at her enthusiasm, and thought she was being a little pushy, but sort of nice in a way. I also admit being on the ranch day after day without any adult female companionship had made me lonely.

I swallowed. "Well, I guess it'd be all right. How about next Tuesday at 9:30?"

"Great! Then it's settled. My class and I will hike over and meet you at the back gate," she said, as she waved good-bye and jogged off down the road.

That evening over a late supper, I casually mentioned to my tired husband, Ranger Ron, about the teacher and her class wanting to come to the ranch on Tuesday. He forced a smile at me.

"Marn, whatever you want to do. I'm sure my boss won't mind, as long as it doesn't cost the open space anything, and you're careful nobody gets hurt."

Money had become a big factor back in 1978. Only a few months earlier Paul Gann's Proposition 13 tax initiative in the State of California passed. As a result, it severely reduced state and local park operating budgets by one-third. There was no money for supplies, additional manpower, materials or mistakes, and Ranger Ron was fast earning the title of "Scrounge Artist."

Over the weekend, I studied the notes I'd taken after Dan Borges told me stories about his family's history and his experiences as a cattle rancher. My work at Petrified Forest National Monument in Arizona, as a naturalist, included giving tours.

But I still felt unprepared on Tuesday morning when a herd of thirty excited, unruly fourth graders charged hell-bent down the hill behind the ranch toward the back gate. I raced out of the mud room door to meet them. Through a thick dust cloud, I could make out their teacher staggering behind them, blowing frantically on her whistle. As she neared the gate, she blew another powerful blast, which immediately signaled the geese, chickens, horses and dogs to start a noisy barnyard ruckus.

I raised my arms at the kids and yelled, "Stop!" Two boys almost crashed into the gate as they skidded to a halt in front of me, while the rest of the class slowed to a moderate trot. A red-headed boy asked breathlessly, "Are you the ranger's wife? Our teacher told us that you would show us around your ranch. Is that your horse?"

As I opened the gate to let the class come in, I calmly answered the boy's questions. "Yes, I'm the ranger's wife, and no, the horse isn't mine. He's the rancher's." The other kids turned an ear, and soon I captured their attention.

"A red and white bull made a loud snorting noise at us when we were on the trail. Does he belong to this ranch?"

A boy wearing a red sweatshirt spoke, "Yeah, Mark said all bulls are mean and will charge you if you're wearing red."

"That's not true," I said. "Most bulls are color-blind and move very slowly."

"So, how come he made a loud snort at us?" a girl asked.

"Probably to let you know that you bothered him."

The kids followed me through the gate. At the stoop in front of the milk house, I sat them down until their teacher caught up. When the rest of the class finally arrived, I told them the story of how Dan Borges' grandfather, Frank Borges, his wife Mary, and their five children first came to the ranch at the turn of the century. "Imagine what it would be like to have to sell off everything you owned to get here, travel for days by wagon over rough dirt roads, haul your water from a creek, and live in a small cabin until you could build a real home," I said. Some of the kids said it might be fun, like camping out. But most of them agreed it would be hard work.

From there, I took them over to the windmill, where each child pumped water from the lift pump and helped me water the cactus, trees and flower boxes.

After we finished pumping and watering the plants, I told the teacher that I hadn't finished feeding all the farm animals before the class arrived.

"Perhaps your students would like to help me feed the calves?"

They all wanted to help. I picked up the grain bucket and headed toward the barn. The class and teacher followed after me, through the corral gate and up to the barn. On our way, I pointed out the Borges longhorn steer brand on the crest of the barn. I asked them if anyone knew what a brand was. I saw several blank faces.

Then one boy spoke up. "Isn't it a rancher's way of telling whose cow is whose?"

"Yes, very good," I said. "A brand is sort of like the cow's license plate. The rancher burns it into the cattle's flesh with a branding iron. It doesn't hurt the cow much, because a cow's hide on the rump or shoulder is almost three-fourths of an inch thick."

I told them that Dan Borges' father, Albany Borges, had introduced the longhorn steer brand when he ran the ranch, and that Dan's grandfather Frank never needed a brand. He only cut a section out of his cattle's ears as a way of identifying them.

I opened the barn door and we crowded into the small space reserved for the calves in front of the alfalfa bales. The smell of fresh alfalfa, damp straw and fresh cow manure in the barnyard made their noses twitch. Several students commented on the potent smell and held their noses. I was so used to the smell, I didn't even notice. But the students soon changed their tune when I opened the back door and let the calves come in.

Immediately three black and white Holstein calves rushed toward me. They nuzzled me with their wet pinkish-white noses and rubbed their curly heads against my thighs, showing their affection. I told the children that they were orphans or drop calves. "Their mothers had died or couldn't take care of them," I explained, "so I'm their mother."

While I went into the small enclosed shed within the barn to fill the calf buckets with warm water and a cup and a half of powdered suckle, the children crowded around the calves and petted them on their backs. "Watch your feet," I hollered. "Don't let the calves step on them."

I brought the buckets full of the warm suckle out of the storage shed and put them in three of the cut-out holes in the calf milk bar along the wall. Seeing the pails, the little calves pushed and shoved their way toward the pails through the crowd of squealing children. They quickly found the nipples and started sucking. I told the kids that most calves are taught by their mothers to suck. But since these calves didn't have mothers, it was up to the rancher and me to show them how. I dipped my thumb into the milk suckle and put it in a calf's mouth. The calf immediately began sucking on my thumb and fingers. "Once a calf gets the idea of how to suck, we put him on the nipple," I said.

The calves drank greedily. When the pails were almost empty, they nudged the bottoms with the tops of their noses under the milk bar. This made the children laugh. I explained, "Calves nudge their mothers' udders to get them to release more milk. It's a natural instinct." The students wanted to know what the word "instinct" meant. I told them that it is a knowledge most animals, including humans, are born with.

After I rinsed out the pails, I let the children climb up into the loft on top of the hay bales. The children soon decided they'd practice jumping from the bales. I worried that one of them was going to twist an ankle, so I laid down the rules. At first, I asked them politely to stop jumping and sit down; then when they ignored me, I found myself shouting at them, "Stop jumping from the bales! Sit down!" Seeing I was wasting my time, I opted just to stand there with a stern look on my face.

Their teacher soon got the message. "Sit down, children, and be quiet!" she demanded. Quickly they obeyed her and found a bale to sit on.

"Listen real hard, and tell me what you hear," I

said. Some said they heard the wind whistling through the eaves, birds, and a faint rustling sound.

When they were all quiet, I told them a story, which I entitled "Large Enough for a Bear."

In the fall when my daughters were about ages three and ten, we noticed that every afternoon for a week, the dogs visited the barn and stayed there two to four hours. We began getting curious, so one afternoon we headed for the barn and just as we started opening the barn door, our two dogs came dashing out with their tongues hanging out, looking as if they'd been drawn through a knothole. Taking our cue from the frightened dogs, we decided to wait before venturing into the barn. After a couple of days, we felt brave enough to investigate. But for protection, we took the smarter of the two dogs with us, and locked the other one up in the shed.

We carried with us a burlap sack large enough for a small bear, a broom and a pitchfork. The dog led the way and we timidly followed. We crept toward the bales of hay and cautiously surveyed them. We wondered if that was where we should begin our hunt for the mysterious intruder.

"Well," said one of my daughters, "we'll soon find it, whatever it is." We then took two hay hooks and rolled a bale over that the dog was sniffing. There was nothing beneath it.

"Humpf," we all said at once.

Over went another bale and another one without finding anything. Finally we heard a soft rustling sound and listened carefully, making sure where the noise originated. Then with the help of my younger daughter Kim, we held the sack open in front of the bale we'd pinpointed. My other daughter Kristin stood behind us armed for battle with the broom. Then the unseen monster began making a piercing, squeaking sound and frantically flying all over the barn, bumping against bales of hay and the support beams. It looked like it would knock itself out. My oldest daughter, who held the broom, began randomly swatting and swinging at the air.

Then the flying "whatever it was" lighted on a bale of hay right in front of us. We quickly opened the sack, which was large enough for a bear, and clamped it over the critter. We opened the bag ever so slightly and peeked inside. In the bag we spied a scared small brown and black creature, with huge mouse ears, a mouse tail and floppy sheet-rubber-black wings. At our embarrassment and the relief that we had finally caught our prey, all three of us burst out laughing, then sadly whined, "Ohhhh. . . poor thing." We carefully put the gunny sack down and turned it inside out. The small bat escaped and flew straight for the open window.

The school children clapped after I finished my story, with the exception of one small boy with watery eyes who just said, "Can we get down now? My hay fever is really bothering me."

From the barn, the kids followed me to the woodpile, where I showed them how to cut up firewood with the two-man saw. "The art of sawing is called bucking. If the blade bends, it bucks like a bucking bronco horse and won't cut," I said. "You don't need muscles to cut up the wood, just rhythm and coordination." Soon they got the hang of it, and all of them wanted to try their hand at cutting the wood.

After the woodpile we visited Honey Bear, the horse. Honey Bear was happy to see the children and trotted right over to the fence, so they could see her up close. I let them feed her some grain with their hands held out flat, fingers tightly closed. Some of the students didn't like it because the horse slimed them with her wet saliva, but the horse loved the attention. The children asked if they could help me groom her, so I showed them how to use the curry comb and brushes, and pull the hair in her tail away from the burr, instead of pulling the burr from the hair.

We then went inside the horse barn, where Dan Borges kept more sacks of grain and bales of alfalfa and wheat hay. "Now, rub your hands together and tell me what you feel," I asked. They said, "Heat." I asked them what caused the heat. There was a silence, then one of the girls said, "I know. Friction."

"Very good," I said. I then explained that we feed the farm animals alfalfa in the winter months when it is cold, because the animals' digestive systems worked harder to digest the alfalfa, creating more friction and heat to keep them warm. In the warmer spring and summer months, we feed the animals wheat hay, which takes less digestive action and creates less heat, so the animal stays cooler, I explained.

I introduced the class to Henry, Ron's pet black and white Plymouth Rock rooster. Henry ate some grain from my hand, then strutted and crowed for them. One kid made a sudden movement that startled the rooster. Henry flew to the top of the woodshed, where he roosted and let out a loud "cock-a-doodle-doo." The entire class burst out laughing.

They then followed me down to the small animal corral, where the children could pet the goats, rabbits, and lambs. The kids got a big kick out of the pigs' antics. The pigs became excited and began snorting and running around their pen. This made the children laugh. The teacher told me they had just finished reading *Charlotte's Web* by E.B. White, so they could really relate with pigs. Cookie and Oreo were regular hams.

I managed to catch Henrietta, a Rhode Island Red hen, who was quite tame, and held her wings tight to her body and covered her eyes with my hand for a moment to calm her down, so that the children could pet her. "Always pet an animal, especially a chicken, in one direction towards the tail, because if the feathers get ruffled and the shafts bent, the nutrients can no longer get through the feather, and the feather in a short time will die and fall out," I said.

I asked where our eyes were located, and where the chicken's eyes were. They said our eyes were in the front of our heads, and the chicken's were on the sides of its head. I then asked them to feel the sun on their cheeks. I told them it was a good day for laying eggs and that the chicken sensed that too. "The sun hits a nerve in the chicken's eye, that goes to the pituitary gland at the base of the chicken's neck," I said. "The gland releases a chemical which goes to the chicken's brain that tells the chicken that it's a good day to lay an egg. It's kind of like a chicken's radio and receiver."

Next, I took the kids to see the Borges children's keepsake wall. They delighted in seeing and touching all the Borges family sayings and curios, especially grandma's comb and grandpa's glasses. The last stop was the two-holer outhouse. One of the students made a big thing about the dual accommodations.

"You mean, more than one person went to the bathroom at the same time? Yuck!"

I told her, "Sure. If you had six kids in the family and all of them took castor oil before they went to bed, there'd be a line-up waiting to use the outhouse the next morning.

"At the turn of the century," I continued, "outhouses were a way of life. People didn't miss the nice indoor bathrooms of today, because they didn't know any difference. The same held true for running water and electricity."

I explained that people tried to keep their out-houses clean, the best they knew how. They moved the "little house behind the big house" to a different location when the hole filled up, poured Clorox bleach and cut lemons down the hole, sprinkled lime powder on the smelly stuff, and put yeast in the hole to eat it up.

"People used to whitewash their houses, fences, chicken roosts and outhouses with lime powder mixed with water, instead of paint, to control the mice and insects," I said. "The lime powder wasn't poisonous, but it tasted bitter, and once it dried, it left the boards clean and white, just like when Tom Sawyer painted the fence."

I told them the story about Mary Borges when she visited Fanny Bancroft and had to use her out-house. Mrs. Bancroft had not only whitewashed her outhouse with lime powder, she'd tucked ging-ham curtains up and flowers in it. When Mrs. Borges came out of the outhouse, she exclaimed, "My, my, Mrs. Bancroft, ain't you gettin' hoity toity lately."

Time was getting short, so we ended the tour by walking around the old house. The children asked if there had been a fire. I told them no. The house was just old, and the boards on it had turned dark weathering over the years. One kid said the house looked like a ghost house because of the paneless black windows. "I've never seen any ghosts, and whenever I walked near the house it only gave me a good feeling," I replied. "With six children living in it, it was probably a happy house." I told the children it was my dream to someday see the house restored to what it looked like around 1910 when Frank Borges and his family lived there. They liked the idea.

The children thanked me for the tour, and the teacher handed me $10. I told her I didn't want any money, but she insisted, and said it was well worth it. I thanked her and said I would put it toward animal feed.

Nonprofit

That one tour snowballed. Within a week, the phone started ringing off the hook, with teachers and scout leaders requesting tours of the Borges Ranch. Ron, supportive of my efforts, said, "Marn, if it's what you want, go for it."

But eventually more requests came than I could handle. One afternoon I told a friend of mine about how swamped I was, and she said, "Look, I have some time I could give to conduct some tours, and my neighbor might also be interested, if you teach us."

Soon the three of us were conducting tours almost every day. Each tour group donated money for our time, and pretty soon the coffee can under my bed began overflowing, so we started a bank account. I wanted us to be legal, so I called the IRS office, and they referred me to the State Office of Historic Preservation in Sacramento. The state office was interested in the ranch. They thought what we were doing was a good idea and suggested that we start a nonprofit organization if we accepted donations, grants and fees. They also advised that we look into putting the ranch on the National Register of Historic Places to protect it. It sounded like a lot of work.

At the time, I was taking a class at Diablo Valley College. I told my instructor I conducted tours for school children, and about our money situation. He liked the idea of starting a nonprofit organization, and told me I could earn four units of credit through a work-study program offered at the college by doing the initial paperwork to become a nonprofit organization.

I presented my plan to the open space specialist, Bob Pond. Bob favored the idea, especially since the Open Space Advisory Committee had recently been dissolved. He agreed to be my mentor and even offered me a corner in the open space office to work on the project. He said if I did all the ground work and initiated the paperwork, including a draft of the bylaws, he would arrange to have an attorney friend of his look over the final paperwork before submitting it to the state and federal governments for approval. My project also included a history of the ranch. This part was fairly simple, since I had already accumulated so much material and stories.

After talking with the Secretary of State's office in Sacramento, I sent away for the forms for becoming a nonprofit organization, using my own personal check. I couldn't believe the amount of paperwork involved. I really had my work cut out for me. After weeks of research and work on the papers, the initial paperwork was completed and ready for final inspection by the attorney. He noted that the forms were all in order and that I had done a good job at providing the needed information. The papers were then sent to Sacramento for final approval, and I got an A in my class.

Approximately six months passed before we heard anything from the State of California. When the approval finally came we were overjoyed, to say the least. Our next step would be to receive nonprofit status from the federal government. Again we filled out the necessary paperwork and waited for a response. Another couple of months went by until the determination letter finally arrived. With the receipt of this letter, the Walnut Creek Open Space Foundation became a viable nonprofit organization.

As the acting executive secretary, I arranged for our first meeting of the foundation. It was a rainy night in February 1979. The open space specialist, Bob Pond; Ranger Ron White; Gary Ginder, who was on the original advisory committee; his attorney friend, Bob Jasperson, who had looked over the paperwork; Hardy Miller; two other people, whose names I can't remember, and I met in the living room of our small house in front of a warm fire.

Guaranteed Protection

We started charging nominal fees for our educational programs, and with the funds paid for interpreters' fees, animal feed, program supplies, special events, a newsletter, display items, and materials for special open space projects. In addition to tours, we offered a three-day/one-overnight living history program for fourth and fifth graders, where students learned to make bread, jam, butter in an old fashioned churn, and stuff sausage. Included within the three days were farm chores, a nature study program, weaving and spinning, blacksmithing, a campfire program, and art. We also offered individual classes in weaving and spinning, nature study, Native American study, art, and cornhusk doll making. All of these programs became popular with the schools and are still going strong today.

Sunset magazine wrote a lengthy article on the ranch. "Evening Magazine," "Bay Area Back Roads," and the "Big Valley" series shot segments of their television programs at the ranch. We co-sponsored with the City of Walnut Creek the annual Borges Ranch Day in June and the Holiday

60

Hoedown in December.

We were earning a name for ourselves, but I was still concerned about the future of the Borges Ranch. I wondered if the buildings would some day be torn down and destroyed. I wanted to protect them for future generations to see.

Once again, I contacted the Office of Historic Preservation. "The only way to guarantee absolute protection is to have the ranch put on the National Register of Historic Places," I was told. Getting the Borges Ranch on the National Register was not going to be an easy task. In 1981, not many people knew about the Register, but I was determined to save the ranch.

With Bob Pond's consent, I sent a check to the Office of Historic Preservation with a letter requesting that an application be sent to us.

It took nearly half a year to gather the needed historical background information, research previous owners, and locate original survey maps. My local hangout became the county offices in Martinez and the county library. I even made a special trip to the University of California at Davis to browse through their historical archives. I conducted oral interviews with Borges family members and picked Dan Borges' brain for every family story he could remember. Eventually, I had gathered enough material to fill a book about the ranch and some wonderful interpretive material.

The original teacher who came to the ranch requesting a tour for her class read the historical piece I had written. She was thrilled with it, and immediately set up an interview with an editor at the Contra Costa Times to publish the manuscript. The interview lasted only ten minutes and the newspaper eagerly offered to print an historical booklet on the Borges Ranch. The booklet became popular with teachers and the public, and we charged $3 per copy to perpetuate the making of more.

With a professionally done historical booklet, a completed application, copies of survey maps and the necessary forms to be placed on the National Register, the open space specialist, Bob Pond, personally hand-delivered our Register packet to the Office of Historic Preservation in Sacramento.

Several months went by before we heard. Then one day in 1981, Bob, acting as liaison, received word from the nominating committee in Los Angeles that the Borges Ranch had been accepted on the National Register of Historic Places.

Fewer than a hundred historical places across the nation had been accepted at that time. It was exciting to be Walnut Creek's first nationally recognized historic site. Even Mt. Diablo State Park and Shadelands Ranch were not on the Register. Bob insisted on driving to Los Angeles to accept the honor at a special luncheon. I wished I could have gone with him, but I wasn't a city employee. An article came out in the Contra Costa Times and more people became interested in the Borges Ranch.

Within a few years, Mt. Diablo State Park and Shadelands Historical Museum in Walnut Creek followed suit and were also placed on the National Register.

Rain Brings Out the Dogs

One morning after a rainstorm, Ron was fixing fences, and I was in the house washing dishes when I heard a terrible squawking coming from the hen house. Kim, now five, screamed, "Mommy! There's three dogs chasing our chickens." I immediately ran outside brandishing a broom at them and shouted, "Get away from my chickens, you chicken nappers! Get out of here before I. . ."

A wet, mud-caked Irish setter had one of my prized white Leghorn hens limply drooping from its mouth. A stream of bright red blood seeped from the chicken's head. I shouted again at the dogs, "You darn dogs! I'll get you for this." The leader, an Irish setter, just stared at me for a second with the chicken in his mouth, then made a mad dash for the gate, with the other two dogs, a yellow lab and a dirty white poodle, right behind him. I couldn't believe it, a poodle. Their flight took them up the road toward the closed back gate, where they found they could not get out.

At the gate, I cornered the setter, where I stupidly grabbed for his collar. He dropped the dead chicken, then growled at me, but didn't make any attempts to bite. I think he was surprised that I would stand up to him. I dragged that dog by the collar back to the house, and the other two dogs followed. After locking the three thieves in the mud room, I called Animal Control. The phone was busy, as usual. After the third try, I called the lost-and-found pet number. A woman answered and said all the lines at the animal shelter were busy. "Call the Sheriff's office," she said. The Sheriff's office told me that they didn't respond to dog problems and to keep trying the Animal Control officer. I could feel a hot red flush creeping up my face as I disgustedly hung up the phone.

I looked through the glass window of the kitchen door at the dogs in the mud room. All three chicken snatchers were lying down, calmly panting with their tongues lolling out. I got brave and gave them a bowl of water. As I was putting the bowl down, the yellow lab trotted over to me and tried to be friendly. I noticed he didn't have a collar; neither did the poodle. Then the setter followed suit. The setter had a phone number on his collar, so I decided to call it. A young man answered, "Hello."

"Ah, do you have an Irish setter?"

"Yes."

"Well, he and two other dogs chased and killed one of my chickens this morning. I have them locked up here at the Shell Ridge ranger station. Can you come get yours?"

"Well, Ma'am, he really isn't mine. He's my brother's, and my brother's out of town for the weekend. He won't be back until late tomorrow. I had the dog tied up in the backyard, but I guess he got loose and jumped the fence."

"Look, I don't care whose dog he is. If someone doesn't come get him in the next twenty minutes, I'm calling the pound!"

I hung up the phone feeling my face flush red again. Just then I heard Ron's truck coming through the gate and Dan's right behind it. I rushed out of the house eager to tell them my misfortune, but immediately realized from their expressions and brusque manner that they were in no mood to listen, especially Dan.

"Ron! We've got to do something about these dogs. This is the second steer I've lost this month. And I'm sure it just wasn't the one dog I shot. There's got to be a pack of them out there to do that much damage. That's almost $1,500 we're talking about." Dan motioned to the back of the truck.

I went around to the back of his pickup. In it was a dead Black Angus steer, its ears bloody and chewed off, with its gray swollen tongue hanging out to the side. Its hindquarters had also been ripped up.

A squirming mess of maggots infested the red, oozing wound. Next to the steer was a lumpy looking burlap sack, with the dead dog inside. This time, when I felt the sting of bile coming up in my throat, I swallowed hard.

"Ah, Dan, you know that pack of dogs you'd

like to get? Well, I think I have them in my mud room. If it's any consolation, they also killed one of my chickens this morning."

El Toro

About 2:30 one Saturday afternoon the phone rang. It was the Walnut Creek police asking if Ranger Ron was available to respond to a call. Ron was out working on a new pigpen, so I put the police dispatcher on hold and hurried outside to yell for him. "Ron! Ron! It's the police and they want you to. . ."

A disgruntled voice from the pigpen yelled back, "What is it this time? Can't you handle it?"

"But, but, Ron, it's the police. They say there's a bull out on Ygnacio Valley Road and they need your help!"

"Tell them I'll be there in a minute."

Within a few minutes, Ron banged open the screen door to the mud room, sweaty, dirty and grinding his teeth because of the interruption. I handed him the phone and tuned in to snatches of the conversation: "A bull is out. . . Rancher is not available. . . They can't get him to go back through the fence. . . need help. . . I see. Tell them I'll be there in a few minutes."

Ron sighed and looked at me. "Marn, I could probably use your help. Get some baling wire and a pair of wire cutters, while I put my uniform and badge on."

When we arrived at the scene, four nervous police officers, fearing they might get their uniforms dirty, an Animal Control officer and two newspaper reporters were frantically waving their arms and screaming obscenities at a young red and white bull who had sinned by innocently wandering onto the road through a break in the fence. Ron stifled a laugh and calmly came to their rescue.

He explained to the officers that they had to slowly move in on the bull as a unit, and think like a bull. "If you were peacefully munching grass along the roadside, minding your own business, when an unexpected blast of sirens split your eardrums and an army of uniformed maniacs rushed toward you waving their arms in the air, your first reaction would be to charge."

As if on cue, the scrappy juvenile sashayed from

side to side, building up steam like a boiler, angrily pawing the ground. He then snorted a vaporous spray from his flared nostrils. Fuming at injustice, the young bull charged Ron head on, ready to pulverize anything that got in his way. Fearing for his life, Ron darted behind a small tree, which seemed much too frail a protection against an oncoming freight train, but enough deterrent to give him a brief moment to make his escape.

Confused by the interference of a foreign object, the bull came to an abrupt stop, eyeing the new opponent. He then charged, flattening the small tree, leaving nothing but a trampled mass. In that brief moment, Ron bolted for the cut section in the fence with the bull following in hot pursuit. Once through the opening, with help from the officers, Ron secured the break, and the bull, safely back in his own confines, was beaten at his own game.

Brian Murphy

RED-TAILED HAWK likes open woodlands, but can be seen in all types of land habitats. Its length is from 19 to 26 inches; a typical wingspan measures 4½ feet.

A Change of Pace

It was a warm spring day in March. After two hours of mucking out the barn, I anticipated a promised walk on Shell Ridge with Kim. So, toting knapsacks loaded with peanut butter sandwiches, binoculars, plant and bird books, we hiked on up over the hill behind the cow barn through a refreshing canopy of valley oaks.

Kim danced on ahead in front of me, picking up treasures of oak galls, pebbles and leaves. As we came out of the shade, the warmth of spring sunshine warmed our backs and inspired us to sing one of Kim's favorite songs to the tune of "Battle Hymn of the Republic."

Little Peter Rabbit had a fly upon his nose,
Little Peter Rabbit had a fly upon his nose,
Little Peter Rabbit had a fly upon his nose,
So, he flipped it, and it flew away.

We followed the trail straight ahead until reaching Twin Ponds, two man-made stock ponds separated in the middle by a dirt levee. The high water made it fun to walk between the ponds and pretend we were crossing a bridge.

Kim found a small branch and started stirring up

the mud at the water's edge, turning the clear water murky. Pointing to something in the water, she squealed, "Look, Mommy, a snake's in the water."

I looked to where she was pointing, and to my amazement, a little green and black garter snake glided across the smooth surface of the water, leaving gentle ripples as it swam. It eased its way across the still pool, then slithered up the bank into the tall green grass.

Hungry, we untied the jackets from our waists, spread them out on the soft grass and sat near a large spreading oak tree. As we wolfed down our sandwiches, then munched pieces of crisp apple, we listened to birds chatter and watched a black and white magpie flit from one tree to another. Bees buzzed in the clover and black sage perfumed the air.

While Kim busied herself lining up pebbles in neat rows, I lay back in the grass and watched billowy white clouds sailing in an azure sky. How lucky we were, I thought, living in an area where folks with foresight set aside beautiful land for all to enjoy. Where, in spring, wild mustard yellows the fields and buckeye sends out vibrant green shoots. On thick velvet grass blacktail deer move casually, browsing on tender young leaves. Stock ponds swollen with winter rain overflow muddy banks pocked by the hooves of cattle. The naked oaks clothe themselves with leafy greenery that casts lacy shadows with the setting sun. Spring sunshine soothes your chilled bones, telling you it is time to don hiking boots. Just around the corner Blue Dicks, California poppies, Chinese Houses, Penstemon, yellow monkey flower and orangish Fiddlenecks will expose their showy heads.

By the first of May, most of the wildflowers start wilting and the grass turns again the golden brown of summer. But then Indian Valley takes on a new hue when the Boy and Girl Scouts hold their annual Camporee and Jamboree and natural colors are swamped in a sea of orange, blue and yellow nylon pup tents.

I lay back in the grass again and closed my eyes. Something tickled me under the chin. I opened my eyes to find Kim kneeling over me tickling my chin with a blade of grass. "Wake up, Mommy, let's go home."

"I must have dozed off. Was I asleep very long?"

"Not very long, but I want to go back now."

"Okay, honey, we'll go." We gathered up our things and headed back down the trail toward the ranch. Ron greeted us when we got back.

"Have a good walk?"

"Yes, Daddy. Look what I found." Kim drew out of her pocket six round pebbles and an aging oak gall. "Mommy said I could keep them. Can I show them to Sister?"

"Yes, Kim."

HERE I AM with my husband Ranger Ron in a photo taken by George Barber early in the year 2000.

Morning

When I was in my thirties, my day started at 6 a.m. when I took my gingham apron off the hook and tied it routinely behind my back. Back then, however, I had more energy.

I remember switching on the radio for the morning news and weather report. Before we bought a satellite dish, we groused about lousy TV reception and rarely watched it. "Temperatures will range in the high nineties today, cooling tomorrow. . ." "President Carter has just announced. . ." At night, instead of watching Johnny Carson, we switched on the radio, climbed into bed and listened to "The Lone Ranger" or "The Shadow Knows."

From our own pigs I sliced bacon off a slab with a large butcher knife and gingerly dropped it into a large black iron skillet to sizzle. From a bowl on the counter, I collected fresh eggs from our own hens and cracked them into the skillet next to the bacon and leftover spuds. The eggs looked so pretty when served on a plate, with their whites firmly nestled around rich yellow yolks. Not at all like store-bought eggs, whose whites spread out and yolks ran all over the pan.

The smell of fresh coffee brewing on the back burner, mixed with the smells of bacon and sweet cinnamon buns in the oven, made any mouth water. I remember slicing oranges, pears, apples or whatever fruit was in season. The plump purple figs that grow on the old fig tree still taste sweet and juicy, but now I mainly let the birds and sheep eat them. These days, at age forty-seven, I drink instant decaf and crunch down a bowl of Kellogg's Special K to keep my weight and cholesterol down.

But I'm still the first one up in the morning. With bare feet, I enjoy softly padding about the house like a cat, while everyone else is asleep. The quiet gives me a tranquil time when I enjoy sipping tea from a china cup, or coffee or hot chocolate from a mug, while curled up in the rocker snug in a thick terry cloth robe.

Sometimes I just study the twin-like photograph in the antique gilt frame of my grandmother and her sister taken in 1898 at ages six and eight; or dust with lemon wax the hand-crafted wood, smooth marble top and black bauble handles of the commode that my great-great-grandfather carried in the back of a covered wagon all the way from Ohio to Oregon in 1853 along the Lewis and Clark Trail. Other quiet mornings I enjoy reading, writing poetry, playing the organ, looking out the window at the bird feeder, or working in the gardens.

But my favorite part of each morning starts when I go on my daily round of feeding the farm animals. Sometimes when I work in the city offices downtown, or when my hip that developed arthritis in it after a bad fall bothers me, Ron or the maintenance people feed them; and although I appreciate their help, somehow I feel cheated. I've always wondered if the animals miss me, too. I look forward to hearing the rooster chorus crowing, wild turkeys gobbling, geese cackling, sheep baaing and the horse whinnying for her breakfast. Einstein, our Polish rooster, with his punk rocker hairdo, is a regular ham at crowing and strutting along the fence rail. The shepherd dogs and labs we've had over the years follow along after me making their fresh marks at various key spots around the ranch. Next comes the horse barn with its fresh smells of alfalfa, chicken scratch, molasses, grains, and horse manure from the nearby corral. From a bale of alfalfa I break off a flake and a half each to throw through the sliding wooden window to Honey Bear and Dan's horse, Tuffy. On winter days I also give them a couple of scoops of rolled oats and corn mixed with molasses.

I break off two more flakes for the five sheep and goats. While I fill two green pickle buckets with day-old bread and corn scratch for the geese, turkeys, laying hens, roosters and wild things, a maverick Rhode Island Red hen and her fancy cock wait patiently for their personal handout. I then fill a coffee can with rabbit pellets for Brownie, Spot and Easter. Back and forth I go carrying the alfalfa

flakes, buckets of grain and bread to the various animals.

When I carry the alfalfa for the sheep, they meet me at the gate and follow me down to their feeding bin, affectionately brushing against me with their soft woolly backs. Jellybean, a black-faced Suffolk lamb, comes up to me trustingly, sniffs the back of my hand, then suddenly shakes her head and jumps away with a start. It makes me laugh. I wonder if it's the smell of the Dial soap I use. The ewe that gave birth to Jellybean actually carried three lambs, one full size and Jelly's runt twin. About a week before the ewe was due to give birth, some kids chased her and she started going into false labor. When the lambs were born the day before Easter, two of them were dead. The one surviving lamb was so small it couldn't reach its mother's teats, so for about five weeks we fed it suckle with a baby bottle. Nancy, one of the maintenance workers who grew up on a dairy farm, squeezed some of the sticky colostrum milk from the ewe the first week. We mixed it with the lamb suckle or formula, so that the lamb could get some natural antibodies.

One day, while I was sitting down in the pen feeding the lamb with the bottle, her mother came over and bit me on a tender part of my hand. Although sheep's teeth are mainly for cropping grass and chewing cud, they can really pinch and break the skin. I smacked that ewe across the nose, and from then on she understood that her lamb needed two mothers if it was going to survive.

George Barber

VISITOR feeds one of the 4-H Club members' goats in a ritual that rates as one of the favorite activities of the day.

George Barber

Magic Hour
by Marnie White

Waxen sun falls
like a half cantaloupe
on the crest of the hills

Bantam rooster balances on a branch
of the locust tree
cocks his head to one side
and crows

The scarecrow in the garden
takes a breath

The clop of horses' hooves
on the wooden floor of the barn
tells me they are hungry

In the water trough
I see the sun
a sliver of amber-colored soap
melting
until there is only
glossy black of night

*   *   *   *   *

Hardly a Drop of Blood

The animal knew me well and would come running when I neared the gate. But the fateful time arrived—a chilly, overcast day in September. Dan Borges, his son Dan, Jr., my husband Ron, a Mexican fellow named Juan and I stood in rubber boots in the wagon shed. Hoses, wash pan and razor-sharp knives were laid out in readiness. Dan's son, with a rifle loaded with .22 longs, stalked the corral, and the bone-shattering roar of the gun announced that the job was done. With a slash of his knife, he cut the jugular vein, allowing the blood to drain out. The men then dragged the huge black carcass on a pallet up to the shed.

I shivered at the sight of the large steer, who only moments before had stood his ground in the corral and now lay motionless with a stream of dark blood oozing from his mouth and throat. With the creaking of chains, block and tackle, muffled voices, grunts and groans, we hoisted the heavy body up over the large beams that bore the marks of so many other slaughters. The massive carcass swung rhythmically back and forth, back and forth, under its own weight. I felt my own body start to sway. I closed my eyes and tried desperately to hold back the acid taste of vomit creeping into my throat. I shivered and felt the color drain from my body. But I would not turn tail and run. I had promised to help and they were counting on me to slap the flies and yellow jackets away with a rolled-up newspaper. This was my test. I had to prove I had the guts to stick it out in a man's world. I knew I would be laughed at if I didn't.

My head started spinning again, and a knife-like pain shot through the pit of my stomach as I watched them make their circular cuts just above the hooves, then cut the animal's feet and head off with a hacksaw. They worked quickly and it was neatly done. The carcass swung round and round, and the rancher yelled to his son to hold it steady so he could make his precision cut the entire length of the body, spilling out stomach sack, intestines, liver, lungs and heart.

I closed my eyes for only a second, envisioning blood gushing from the incision, but to my surprise, there was hardly a drop. The rancher then skillfully detached the innards from the cavity. He put the liver and heart in a pan of cool water and the rest of the organs in a gunny sack to be given a proper burial later. I then watched them skin the meat. Slowly they peeled back the skin with their sharply honed knives, each cut the same level as the previous one. After they completely removed and scraped the hide, they rolled it up and bound it with baling wire, leaving the brand showing on the outside.

They then washed down the carcass with cold water and quickly pinned a clean white sheet around it so that the fat would not turn yellow. Together we lowered the body and eased it carefully onto the truck bed, where the rancher's son would take it to the butcher.

A yellow jacket lit on my arm and left its vicious sting. I slapped at it wildly.

George Barber

ORIGINAL Borges Ranchhouse serves as the Visitor Center. Built about 1899, it was restored in 1991.

"Tardy Hardy"

Bill Hardy, never on time, but a likable sort of guy, always brought a joke or tale to tell.

The time I met him, he was bending over fitting a shoe to Dan's gelding in front of the barn. Kim, who was seven at the time, and I came over to where he was working.

"Mind if we watch?"

"Nope, just don't get in the way of the horse."

We watched him trim the horse's hoof with a big pair of hoof snips, then clean and cut off the overgrown frog, which is the fleshy part of the hoof. He filed the hoof with a large rasp and sorted through a box of horseshoes looking for just the right fit. Then with calloused hands that had done it a thousand times, he nailed the shoe to the hoof, and filed it once more.

He looked up from his work and said, "Here, want some chewin' gum?" Kim stretched out her hand and quickly pulled it back in disgust when she saw his offering of a piece of gristle from the horse's hoof.

He chuckled to himself, and as if it was part of the act, flipped the scrap of frog to his scruffy dog, who greedily gobbled it up. He then went back to putting the shoes on the horse.

After he finished, he stood up, rubbed his rounded back and said, "You must be the ranger's wife."

Bill, like Dan Borges, was to become a special friend. Many times over the years he shoed and trimmed Honey Bear's hooves, stayed for a cup of coffee and a piece of pie, fed the farm animals when we were gone, helped load hay into the barn, shared his delightful stories, played Santa Claus at our Christmas celebrations, and helped Dan rebuild the horse barn.

Stir Crazy

It had been raining three days straight, so when the weather cleared the day before Thanksgiving, I decided to take Honey Bear out for a romp in the lower pasture.

When I approached her she greeted me with her usual arrogant manner and seemed eager to leave the confines of the corral. She stepped right out and tugged on the lead rope, which I had to hold firmly in my hand. I tied her to the hitching post in front of the tack room, where she moved her head from side to side scanning her surroundings.

"Calm down, girl. What's got you so hyped up today, anyway?"

She stared at me with her big brown eyes, flicked her sensitive ears and let out a long whinny which was immediately answered by Dan's gelding, Tuffy, back at the corral. With a brush and curry comb in my hand, I started removing the mud and dirt from her coat.

Most of the time she liked being groomed and would almost fall asleep because it felt so good, but this day she wouldn't stand still. Soon her clean winter coat felt soft and silky, and I hugged her graceful strong neck. She closed her eyes as her way of saying she liked the attention. But it was an effort to pick her hooves. Usually all it took was a tap on the upper part of her thigh and she would willingly lift a hoof for me, but now she stubbornly balked as I practically pried her feet from the ground. She also kept leaning on me when I worked on them. I then combed out the snarls and burrs from her wispy Appy tail and mane.

"There. Don't you look pretty." She nodded her head in her highbrow fashion as if to say, "Yes, I know. Jealous?" which made me laugh.

I got out the saddle, blankets and bridle. For once she stood still and allowed me to put them on her. I shook out the thick saddle pad and put it over her broad back, then the soft Navajo weave Ron gave me the previous Christmas, then the saddle. I ran my finger across the cantle. I hadn't used any saddle soap on my saddle for a while and knew I had another job to do that week. I then pulled up the cinches and adjusted the stirrups. She kept bloating up on me, so I punched her a couple of times in the side. I then mounted her, testing the saddle. It felt snug and secure. She accepted the bit with no problem. After I unbuckled the halter we started off at a slow walk toward the lower pasture. About half way there, she started doing a "jig." Her rear end bumped up and down and made for an awfully uncomfortable ride.

I yelled, "Stop it, girl!" and pinched her withers

with my thumb and forefinger. She stopped the jigging, then started jerking her head up and down. She finally stopped after a few sharp kicks in the flanks and let me ride her toward the new dam. We checked it out and turned, heading back to the pasture. Just then Tuffy let out a long, lonely whinny from the barn. Honey Bear perked up her ears, snorted and answered him with a long, high-pitched whinny. Then without warning, she bolted and took off at a full gallop toward the barn. I dug my knees into her sides, leaned as far back as I could in the saddle and screamed, "Whoa, girl! Whoa!"

Then as if my words triggered a switch in her brain, she made a dead stop, hunched up her shoulders and threw me as hard as she could. I landed on my head five feet away, then flipped over onto my back. I must have been unconscious at least five minutes before I woke to the dog sniffing me. The horse was nowhere in sight.

I was dazed, and a sharp pain ran from my head to my shoulders. My right eye ached, and I reached a shaky hand to my face. The eye was almost completely swollen shut and I had a huge bump on the top of my head. I closed my eyes again and lay there a minute, while trees and green hills swirled around me. But something in me told me I had to get up and get to the house.

I ran my hands down my legs and they seemed okay. Slowly I rolled over and crawled to a sitting position. A severe pain shot through my body from the base of my neck as I scrambled to get to my feet. Immediately, my legs started shaking. They buckled under me and down I went, exhausted, like an empty feed bag.

"No!" I said, and managed to drag my weakened body forward. Clawing and scratching the dirt, half scooting, I finally reached the ranch house, where my oldest daughter Kristin radioed my ranger husband for assistance.

Ron showed up in about fifteen minutes.

Shocked at my appearance, he helped me into the pickup and we took the shortcut through the open space to Kaiser Hospital. Luckily, no bones were broken, just my pride, but it would be a week before I could get out of bed.

Later that evening, Dan, the rancher, came in to see me.

"Hey, kid, hear ya fell off your rockin' horse. Say, that's too bad. Kinda got bunged up, didn't ya?" Dan then scolded me in his own way for taking the horse out when I should have known she was "stir crazy." Not wanting to make me feel any worse, he added, "Say, did you know she was comin' into heat?"

From that lesson, I learned: Never ride alone, and take early warning signs from animals. Honey Bear is now 25 years old, has had arthritis in her hips for the past five years, and is living out her days in the pasture.

I hadn't ridden much since then. About a month ago, though, Charlie, a cowboy in his eighties, and his friend Burt trailered their four horses over. Ron wasn't at the ranch when they came, so when Charlie asked if I'd like to go riding with them, I jumped at the opportunity. Charlie let me ride his prize cutting horse, Zippo, who had won over $38,000 in prize money. That horse was a Lincoln Continental with power steering. With just a little leg pressure, he'd obey my every command so smoothly, I wasn't even stiff and sore the next day. A few days later over a piece of homemade lemon meringue pie and coffee, I mentioned to Charlie how much I enjoyed the ride. He said we'd have to go riding again, and I told him I just might take him up on it.

That Lady's Got Guts

On a Friday afternoon, Channel 5 called. A producer told us they would be coming out to the Borges Ranch on Monday for background shots for their daily "Evening Magazine" program. Hurriedly, we made a few last-minute phone calls, rustling up some school children to help with a branding demonstration, and Fritz's Meats and Catering of Concord said they'd set up a barbecue. At the appointed time, 11:30 a.m., all was ready. The animals were fed, flowers watered, Fritz had the coals going, and the kids were jumping up and down in anticipation.

Everyone kept checking watches, 11:45, 12:00, 12:30. Finally, at 12:45, a white van with purple and lavender letters reading "Channel 5 KPIX Evening Magazine" pulled into the drive.

A young man bounded from the van, ran up to my husband Ron, the ranger, and gasped, "Wow, did we have a hard time finding this place. Thought we'd never get here. Someone must have given us the wrong directions."

Ron just smiled and nodded. He'd heard the excuse before.

The young man then went around to the passenger side of the van to help Jan Yanehiro, one of the co-hosts of "Evening Magazine." To our surprise, she was very much pregnant; nine months, in fact. My eyes opened wide and I thought, that lady's got guts to be bouncing around the countryside in her condition. We were introduced to her and Richard Hart, her co-host, the director, and our contact person, Faye Lavine.

After a short survey of the ranch, the director said, "We'll shoot the entire opening and closing of the shows for five days all on the same day by taking shots in different spots around the ranch."

We figured from the way the director talked, it would be easy and the whole thing would only take a couple of hours at most, leaving plenty of time to enjoy Fritz's delicious barbecue dinner.

For the first shot, Jan sat on the stoop near the chicken shed flanked by Henry, our big Plymouth Rock rooster, on one side and the calf on the other. Jan timidly took the calf's suckle bottle and was told by the director, "Pretend you're feeding it." She took the bottle and clucked how cute he was when he tugged at the nipple.

Her dress was pieced with a vibrant green, orange and blue that looked like a flashing multicolored neon sign in contrast to the rustic brown of the shed. Even her cowboy hat was the same luminous green.

Later the director told us the co-hosts wear

bright colors because they show up better on TV.

Then everyone was asked to stand back and to keep quiet while Jan and Richard said their opening lines. The director barked, "Take One."

Jan said, "Here we are at the ah-ah-ah. . . Old Bogus?"

"Okay, cut. Take Two," the director interjected.

This time it was Richard's turn to botch his line. You could see the director becoming irritated and impatient. Waving her hands in the air, she sighed, "All right, let's try it again, shall we? Take Three. And make it good. We've only got so much footage."

Luckily, the third shot came out perfect. "Great!" she yelled. "Now, the next shot in front of the wagon wheel near the cactus."

In the meantime, Ron and I herded the school kids over by the cattle chutes for the branding demonstration. Ron pulled out the irons, pill plunger, nose clamp and grease can and we gave each student a role to play. We then went through the motion of branding one of the volunteer mothers.

Rehearsal over, we were all now expert cowhands and ready to be filmed, but what was holding up the camera crew? Fifteen minutes went by. A half hour. The sun was getting hot and sticky, and first-grader attention spans were fast slipping away. Only fifteen minutes left before they had to head back to school.

Finally the camera crew came over and asked us to demonstrate in the background while Jan and Richard spoke. It took two takes to get it right, and I couldn't help feeling sorry for Jan standing with a silver sun reflector beaming directly on her face and the hot sun beating down on her bare head. She looked like she was going to fall over with heat stroke. After the shot, I brought her a glass of ice water. She was grateful and thanked me. She then asked if she might use my bathroom.

The school kids left right after the spot and then the director yelled, "Lunch break!"

I looked at my watch. It was almost three o'clock, and they still had four more segments to shoot.

Fritz's barbecued steak, chili beans, potato salad, green salad, and ambrosia salad delighted all of us. But even this gourmet spread Jan and Richard couldn't thoroughly enjoy. As soon as they sat down, refreshing themselves with a cold Pepsi, the director ushered them over to the barbecue pit and told them, "Pretend you're cooking." While they spoke, smoke blew in their faces and brought tears to their eyes. The director commented, "Oh, what's a barbecue without a little smoke."

Jan and Richard were allowed to eat their meal, but had to do another spot while they were eating. In all, they had only ten minutes of their own time to relax.

After their hurried late lunch, Richard mounted

a horse and pretended he was riding in from the range to give an introduction. During this time, Jan waddled over to the woodpile, where she found a log to sit on, and put her head in her hands. I walked over and asked if she was feeling okay, and if I could get her anything.

She looked up at me with fatigued eyes and said, "Another glass of ice water would be wonderful." I brought her the water and she said, "It tastes good. Thanks." I smiled.

Then she asked, "Your two daughters, how old are they?"

"Six and thirteen," I said shyly. I felt awkward and nervous talking to her, as if entering forbidden ground, especially since she was a celebrity.

"Oh, your oldest is thirteen. You must have had her when you were quite young."

"No, I was twenty-three. I guess to some people that's young. Is this your first?"

"Yes, but I'm thirty-four, really too old for having a baby."

I smiled. "No, you aren't. Thirty-four isn't old. Lots of women these days have babies in their thirties, even early forties, especially if they had a career first."

She smiled and seemed to warm up to me. Then I asked, "How was your trip to China?"

"I was six months pregnant then, but it was interesting, although our hotel accommodations weren't so great."

"Oh?" I said.

"Yes, we didn't have any hot water for the entire two weeks we were there." The director then called Jan back for another take.

Jan and Richard had only two takes left. Then a plug for the San Francisco Civic Arts Food Sculpture Exhibit. Jan held a ceramic horse coated with gold and white glossy jelly beans while Richard tried on a ten-pound cowboy hat also covered with beans. I don't know how they can call an object art by just gluing a bunch of jelly beans onto it. I looked at Jan and Richard, and they looked like they didn't think much of it either.

The last shot was the best. With a background picture of my girls swinging on the rope swing from the walnut tree, Jan and Richard advertised a contest for a temporary replacement for Jan during her maternity leave. The contest rules were simple: Just write in twenty-five words or less why you feel you are qualified to take Jan Yanehiro's place as co-host of Evening Magazine during her absence. The winner gets to co-host the show with Richard Hart for a week.

I couldn't help chuckling to myself—Sucker! I looked at my watch. The time was 6:20 p.m.

Summer Time

In late May the temperature reached a tongue-lolling ninety degrees. The hills overnight turned a crisp pancake brown, the 1916 windmill creaked and turned slowly protesting the lack of oil, and the chickens hovered around the water feeder. Small families of cattle spent their days congregated in the shade of the oak trees, slapping and spatting at the herds of black, biting flies on their backs.

With each bang of the screen door a battalion of pesky barn flies stormed the kitchen, lighting on cupboards and walls or clinging to the repulsive strips of sticky, gooey flypaper hanging from the ceiling. By the end of summer, the cream-colored walls were speckled with a mass of brown fly-specks. A continuous trail of thirsty ants led up the kitchen counter, and mouse turds dotted the white Dove soap bar near the sink.

We started work at 5 a.m. and quit at 2 p.m., looking forward to an afternoon swim. As I headed down the gravel path to the pond, the warm air was thick with the pungent smell of black sage, the bushes rattled with the scurry of ground squirrels, and a two-foot-long brown and black gopher snake slithered across the path in front of me. My skin felt dry and prickly, and I could feel the seep of sweat dampening my breasts.

At the water's edge my stomach squirmed at the thought of easing my feet into the fresh black cow-pie mud. I felt the soft mud ooze between my toes and suck at my ankles, releasing an odor of rotting weeds. With a giant leap, I flopped in the water and dog-paddled to the center of the pond, freeing myself from the hairy grasp of joint grass. I floated on my back, gazing at a rainbow-auroraed sun, dusty beams of sunlight bouncing off reeds and cattails, mirroring an opulence in the water.

Overhead I heard the burr of red-winged black-birds, their black shadow arcing the sun. Circling the pond, they came to rest on the cattails. Their brilliant red shoulder patches lit up the reeds.

NAMED for the first open space specialist, Bob Pond reflects the images of a group of horseback riders.

Dixon Livestock Auction

It was fall again, and the four pigs had reached a whopping 250 pounds each in only five months. I helped Ron load them into the back of the pickup truck, enlarged with plywood boards on either side, the night before the Dixon Livestock Auction. The hogs balked stubbornly, but we coaxed them in with scraps of food. They squealed like babies when we pulled them by their back legs and walked them like wheelbarrows up the ramp into the truck. The biggest pig, Jane, actually cried to get our sympathy. All four knew they had enjoyed a good home for the spring and summer.

It was hard letting them go. We had given two of them names, and they each had their own personalities. Normally we don't name an animal if we know we must sell or butcher it. It makes it easier that way. But the time had come when we could no longer feed them, and already two of them exhibited signs of orneriness.

The next morning we fed the other farm animals before leaving for Dixon. We arrived about eight a.m. The stockyard seethed with pickup trucks, horse trailers, and large rigs with every variety of pig imaginable, and the din of snorting pigs and shouting pig farmers. We looked like small potatoes with only four pigs to our name. Ron parked our pickup truck in line with the others, and went into the office for the necessary paperwork. I clambered out of the truck and checked on the pigs. They were quiet and looked up at me with solemn eyes. I wondered if they knew their fate.

I stared at the multitude of trucks and pickups. Crammed in the back of an old flatbed truck with rough plywood siding must have been close to thirty pigs. I watched the farmer and a teenage boy kick and prod them with long sticks, herding them out. They squealed, grunted, snorted and snapped at each other as they made their way out of the truck through a maze of chutes through a large gate where they were counted and herded into lots of six to nine in small holding pens. In each pen were usually four to six pigs. Some of the pigs, angry and ornery, ran around making a lot of noise, while others, seemingly accepting their fate, lay down. I had never seen or known there were so many different types, sizes and shapes of pigs. I recognized some of the more familiar breeds: black and white Hampshires, pinkish-white Yorkshires, and the red Durochs.

The assortment included an old heavy-bodied sow with teats extended from having a dozen piglets suck on them, and a bristle-backed black and white boar with a long nasty snout and floppy torn ears that looked like an old hound dog's. Some pigs had cut-out sections on parts of their ears, a method of ear marking similar to what Dan did with his cattle. Some sported long curly tails that wagged or stood straight out when they were frightened. Others had tails that had been docked or nipped off by another pig, leaving them with little stubs.

Finally our unloading time came. Ron pulled up to the unloading ramp and opened the tailgate of the pickup. Our pigs hesitated at first, but Ron threw some grain in front of them and they scrambled right out. Then, stinging from the whack of a worker's prod, they ambled down the chutes to the counter, who wrote down the numbers, weight, sex and type of pig on the form Ron had handed him. He signed the form, kept one copy, and gave the other to Ron for his record.

We wandered over to the one cafe on the yard. It was built of scrap plywood and galvanized corrugated iron sheeting from what looked like the 1930s. As we opened the screen door, a battalion of flies buzzed past us. The smell of hot bacon grease, working men's body odor (that I mistook for onion sweat), cigarette smoke, and the smell of pig and cow manure from the patrons' boots permeated the place.

The tables were occupied with farmers drinking coffee, talking and filling their oversized guts with platters of fried eggs, sausage and hash browns, so we sat at the counter.

A sign on the wall read, "Working Man's Special. Your choice—two ranch eggs any style, bacon or sausage, hash browns or biscuits with country gravy. $3.75." A big woman wearing a soiled apron, blue kerchief tied around her hair, and a pot of coffee in her hand, came by. She set two thick-rimmed mugs in front of Ron and me, and started pouring us a cup of coffee before we even said we wanted some. "First cup's on the house," she said. "Whatta ya have, folks?"

Ron looked at the sign on the wall and said, as if he ordered it every day, "I'll have the special, with eggs over easy, bacon, and biscuits with lots of gravy."

After seeing the greasy eggs served to the farmer next to us, Kim and I each ordered a hamburger and Coke.

People milled in and out, talking prices of beef and pork, and smoking cigarettes. With each customer the screen door banged open, causing a dozen more flies to buzz in and settle back against the warm window pane.

The pig farmers wore overalls stained with mud and knee-high rubber boots caked with bits of straw and pig grunt. Their hat styles ranged between cowboy and battered fedoras, soiled around the bands and misshapen.

I sat next to two pig farmers, one telling the other a story about his father's two mules named

Jack and Jenny. Jack was the "gee," and Jenny the "haw."

After some time, the waitress brought Ron's eggs and our hamburgers. The hamburgers were thick, juicy ones on soggy buns, richly lavished with mayonnaise, garnished with a generous slice of purple Bermuda onion, overripe tomato, and slightly brown-edged lettuce. I cut Kim's hamburger in quarters so she could get her mouth around it.

The complimentary french fries were thick, greasy country style, which Kim didn't want because they didn't look or taste like McDonald's. "Put them on my plate," Ron said.

The mustard and catsup were in glass bottles sitting in front of the farmer next to me. He placed his hand on the catsup bottle, even though he wasn't using it.

I turned to him. "Ah, excuse me, sir. Can you please pass me the catsup?"

He turned and gave me a dirty look. "Just a minute, lady. Can't ya see I'm usin' it?" I raised my eyebrows and gave him one of my "give me a break" looks. He then poured a glob on his scrambled eggs and plopped the catsup bottle right down on the counter in front of me. "Here!" he said and continued with his story about the two mules.

I smothered my burger with the catsup, took a large bite and smiled to myself. It was the best tasting hamburger I'd ever eaten.

Afterward we found a seat in the auction area. In the center was a sawdust ring for showing the animals. Bleacher-type benches were placed in a semicircle around the arena. At one end the auctioneer block adjoined an open aisle for the animals. Ron warned Kim and me, "Keep your hands down to your sides. Don't even scratch your noses." This was one way some auctioneers accepted a bid. We promised him that he could do the bidding for us.

The first animals auctioned off were the boars and sows, then the weaners—piglets just old enough to be separated from their mothers.

They brought them in in lots of thirty, eleven, six, and three, then a couple of loners. Toward the end, they brought in a lone red piglet. He looked different from the rest. His hind legs were too long, and his back was arched too high. The ringmaster pushed and prodded him with his cane, persuading him to move. The piglet swaggered like a drunken sailor and stood on wobbly, thin legs, then sat down on his haunches in the center of the ring.

There was a slight laughter. The auctioneer started his prattle, "Oh, come on, gents. Whatta ya give me for this here. . ." He hesitated before saying "pig."

"Do I hear $1.75, 1.50, .50? Will ya give me fifty cents? Who will give me. . ." No one came forth; then Ron timidly raised his hand.

"Sold!" said the auctioneer with a rap of his

gavel. "What's your name, son?"

"White," Ron answered, slightly embarrassed. Later, Ron told me he really didn't want the pig. He just felt sorry for it and raised his hand in hopes someone else might bid on it.

Now that we had a new pig, we wandered over to the cattle auction. A red and white heifer was up for sale. She looked good, no cataracts, coat thick and glossy, and no signs of splay feet.

Ron bravely made a bid of 44 cents per pound.

The auctioneer rattled off, "44, 44, 44, 44, 44, 44, 44 1/4, 45, 5, 5, 45, 5, 5, 5, 5, 5, 5, 5. Do I hear 6, do I hear 6, 6, 6, 6, 6, 6? Sold to White!"

So, we came with four animals and left with two: a young heifer and a poor excuse for a pig so small he fit in a cardboard box bound with rope.

When we reached the ranch, the heifer made herself right at home by greeting the bulls and making her presence known. We took the little critter down to the pen. He looked even smaller in the pen all alone, especially since just the day before, the pen held four good-sized pigs.

He took a drink of water, but only sniffed at the food we put out for him. Later he threw up the water. Ron gave him a shot of "Calmbiotic" to kill stockyard diseases. He bedded him down for the night with an armload of fresh hay.

The next morning we found the pig listless, back legs spastic and flanks sunk in. He looked through glazed eyes and let out a scream for help.

I ran to the house and warmed up a bottle of milk for him.

Two horseback riders, who often asked me to ride with them, came by. They found me sitting cross-legged in the middle of the pigpen with the little critter cradled in my arms, trying to give him a bottle.

"Now, if that don't take the cake," one of them said. "Every time we ride past here, we find you doing something out of the ordinary with your animals. Last time, you had your arm clean up to your elbow inside a ewe, helpin' pull out a dead lamb."

I smiled, then asked them for help carrying the pig to the house, where I gently placed him in the old bathtub on the front porch. The tub made a good crib. Between the three of us we force-fed him some milk and he perked up some. The riders went on their way, and I figured I could give the piglet a second feeding after I finished my chores.

For two solid hours our watch dog stood vigil over the small patient, growling whenever the curious puppy came too close. Later that afternoon I checked on the pig again. I felt sick when I discovered it was dead.

I accepted the death, because I really didn't have my hopes up too high for his survival. The hard part would be telling our seven-year-old daughter Kim when she got home from school. Kim was a tough little kid, though, and it wasn't the first time she'd seen death. She had lived almost her entire life on the ranch and experienced the death of a Black Angus calf born prematurely, Ron's pet Plymouth Rock rooster, Henry, after he'd been kicked in the head by a strange horse in the barn, chickens and rabbits that had expired from the summer heat, even one of Dan Borges' steers, maimed by wild dogs—and now her first little piglet.

About an hour after I told Kim the bad news, I spied her through the kitchen window swinging back and forth on the rope swing Ron had made for her under the English walnut tree in the yard. Later she came in and took my hand. "Mama, come with me. I want to say a prayer for the pig."

I obliged and followed her to the porch, where the pig lay still in the bathtub. I could see it was already starting to get stiff. Next to its body, Kim had carefully placed a ring of violet-colored petunias, yellow marigolds and bright pink geraniums.

Rachel

While I weeded in the vegetable garden, an old white pickup truck rolled in the drive with a cow in the back. As the unofficial greeter at the ranch, I traipsed toward the front gate to find out who was visiting. A gray-haired man in his mid-fifties poked his head out the window and asked, "This the Borges Ranch?"

"Yes, ah. . ."

"Well, I'm Earl Allen and this here's my wife Fern," he said, turning to the petite salt-and-pepper-haired woman sitting by him. She smiled coyly.

"Oh, hello, I'm. . ." I began.

He interrupted by saying, "We've brought our cow, Rachel, over to be bred with Dan Borges' bull. You know where we're supposed to put her?"

"Ah, neither Dan nor Ron are here right now. I'm only the ranger's. . ." I guess my words didn't mean much to him, because he cut in again.

"Where's the loading chute?" I nonchalantly pointed in the direction of the chute and he backed the pickup truck there. He got out, sized it up, shook his head and said, "Nope, that'll never do.

Too high. Got another?"

"No, that's the only one. Maybe you could back up to the side of the hill and let her out."

He didn't particularly appreciate that idea, shook his head again, and went alongside his wife. "Well, we'll just have to force her to jump out."

"No, Earl!" Fern exclaimed. "She might break a leg or something."

"Ah, huh, just get out of the truck, Fern, and give me a hand, will you?" He walked back, lowered the tailgate and removed the restraining boards. Fern kept on whining, "But Earl, she'll get hurt. It's too high."

The cow, Rachel, apparently already resolved the situation, psyching herself up to make the jump, because as soon as Earl lifted the last restraining board off, she scrambled out of the truck bed and on up the slope like it was an everyday occurrence. With a rope tucked around her rump, and a few soothing words from Fern, we soon herded her in the right direction toward the corral gate. I quickly opened the gate. With a few waves of our arms, we cornered her near the back gate of the corral.

Ferdinand, Dan's prize bull, soon caught her alluring scent and ambled over. Standing firm, his massive chest and neck muscles rippled up and down under his ruffled collar of folded skin called the dewlap. The bull then raised his flared nostrils to the wind, catching a better drift. Rachel took one google-eyed look at her future mate and without further ado, trotted right in with the bull.

Ferdinand, a young but experienced bull, wasted no time in being neighborly, and let out a series of jubilant bellows at her presence. Rachel, overjoyed with the whole affair, was soon taken with her new suitor. After all, it wasn't every day that a prized Hereford bull became enamored with a simple Guernsey milk cow.

"See, Earl, I told you he'd like her," Fern said.

"We're sorry for leaving so soon," she continued. "Earl and I have an appointment this afternoon, but will be back this evening to milk the cow."

They piled into the pickup truck and drove off. Dumbfounded, I wondered what I'd tell Dan. I hoped I hadn't been left holding the bag.

Dan didn't show up at the ranch that day. When Ron got home, I told him about the cow. He told me not to worry about it; Dan probably had made arrangements with the Allens before leaving on vacation.

After dinner, I went horseback riding with my friend Sue. I'd just returned and began grooming the horse when the Allen's beat-up truck once again skidded in on the loose gravel by the corral.

Fern climbed out, laden with a milking stool, stainless steel pail, a large glass jar, washcloth and washbowl. I put down my curry comb and scurried over to introduce her to Ron. Fern greeted us with a smile.

"Earl couldn't come. Ah, I was wondering if you might help me get Rachel into the barn so I can milk her."

The way Fern asked, Ron and I expected we'd need the bull whip, but when Ron opened the gate, Fern quietly approached Rachel, spoke softly in her ear, and the cow, like a faithful companion, trotted along behind her into the barn, leaving a poor heart-broken Ferdinand at the corral gate.

Once in the barn, we tied Rachel up and kept her occupied with a flake of alfalfa. Fern placed the small stool by Rachel, sat down on it, and gently washed Rachel's udder and teats with lukewarm water. She placed the empty pail under the cow's udder and gripped the two back teats. She pulled and squeezed them in an up-and-down motion until a stream of warm yellowish milk zinged into the pail. Rachel continued chewing her cud and seemed content with her new surroundings. I studiously watched Fern pull up and down on the teats in a rhythmical motion. Fern sensed my curiosity and in her soft voice asked, "Want to give it a try?"

"Ah, okay, sure," I said nervously. She got up from the stool and instructed me to sit down in her place. "Rub your hands together till they're warm," she said. Then she showed me how to place my hands on the front two teats. They felt warm and rubbery in my grasp. I pulled and tugged, but not a drop of milk came out. Fern laughed.

"She's probably not used to your touch and

tensed up. Relax. Give her a minute. Animals can tell right off the bat if you're nervous, or if you're a greenhorn."

I waited a few minutes. This time when I attempted to milk her, a thin stream of creamy-white milk squirted into the pail.

Fern said, "That's it. Keep it up. You're doing fine. Before you know it, you'll be able to milk her all by yourself."

It was fun helping Fern milk the cow, but after only a short time, my hands ached and I felt tired. Fern noticed my fatigue.

"After a few weeks, your muscles will build up and it will become natural," she said with a strange gentle giggle.

I raised my eyebrow at her comment. Was she setting me up to get me to milk her cow for her? I shook my head and timidly said, "No. I don't think so. I still need a lot of practice."

"Did you know, Rachel hasn't had a calf in six years and still gives a pail full of milk every day? But we want her to have a calf now, so she'll keep on giving milk."

"Wow! I didn't know that," I said.

We put Rachel back in the corral and took the milk into the kitchen, where Fern showed me how to pour the raw milk through paper and cloth strainers, ridding it of any debris such as bits of alfalfa, hair, and dirt. She then poured the strained milk into the large wide-mouthed jar, smiled and proudly asked, "Would you like a taste?"

Ron and I both eagerly reached for a glass. The rich lukewarm milk slid down our throats with ease, leaving a thick buttery coating on our tongues and the roofs of our mouths.

"Mmmmm. It's delicious and so creamy," I commented.

"Yes, Guernseys are noted for having a high butterfat in their milk."

I asked Fern if she pasteurized her milk, which is the process of boiling it to kill germs. She told me that pasteurization started at a time when some folks weren't so careful about keeping things clean. She said that if you watch what your cow eats, wash her teats and udder before each milking, and make sure all your equipment is clean, boiling your milk really isn't necessary if it's for your own use. She also said that it takes all the nutrients out of it.

"Did you know that kids who drink raw milk have fewer allergies? If they have allergies from certain weeds and pollens near their home, they eventually build up a tolerance to them if their cow is allowed to graze in the same area. Did you ever hear of your great grandmother suffering from allergies, like kids today?"

I thought of my own daughter, whose nose ran continuously during the spring months.

"No. Does that work the same as when some people eat raw honey?"

"Yes, the bees collect pollen from the plants

and transfer strains of it through their honey. Course I'm not sayin' it works for everyone. Here, take the milk. I have plenty more at home."

Ron and I looked at each other and graciously said, "Thank you."

"Well, I better be gettin' home. I have lots of things to do and another cow to milk. I'll be back tomorrow evening. Rachel can wait until then to be milked, unless you'd like to try your hand at milkin' her again." She gave me a teasing little smile. I didn't say anything, gave her a forced smile back, and hoped Dan would soon return.

Stark Naked

One morning we were awakened at 3 a.m. to the sound of the dogs barking and someone furiously ringing the ranch hand bell outside our front door. Alarmed, I whispered to Ron to peer out the window before answering the door. He looked, gave sort of a half laugh, half snort, and opened the door. Standing by the gate was a young man about sixteen years old, stark naked.

"Ah, are you okay?" Ron asked, trying hard to keep a straight face.

"Yeah, I think so. This the ranger station?"

"Yes, and it's three o'clock in the morning. What are you doing here?" Ron said, slightly annoyed at being disturbed at such an ungodly hour.

"Oh, I'm sorry. I didn't know what time it was," our visitor said. "Me and a friend were at this party where I ate these mushrooms. At least I think they were, cause some girl came up to me and said, 'I wouldn't eat those mushrooms if I were you.' But I'd already eaten two or three of 'em. Then a little later on, I didn't feel so good, and started actin' really weird.

"So these two guys said they'd take me home in

their car. They'd had a few beers, but could still drive. But instead of takin' me home, they took me to the end of this road, where there was this park. They made me take off all my clothes, then told me to start runnin'. One of 'em pointed his finger at me like it was a gun, and said, 'or we'll shoot!' They were all laughin'. I was scared, and didn't know what to do, so I ran. After a while, I puked my guts out near some bushes. I don't remember much after that. Then I saw your lights and a sign that said, 'Ranger Station.' Please, mister, can you call my dad to come get me?"

The kid was shivering, even though it wasn't cold outside. Ron asked me to get him the rain slicker from the hall closet, and told the kid to sit down on the bench on our porch. Ron sat next to him and asked him for his name and address. Ron nodded as though he recognized the last name.

Under normal circumstances, Ranger Ron probably would have called for a police officer to take the kid to Juvenile Hall, but decided the best thing at such a late hour and because he wasn't feeling very well, was to let him call his father. The kid lived nearby; he didn't appear to be a bad kid, and his story was so outrageous, it was funny. Ron brought the young man into the kitchen and showed him the phone.

"Hello. . .Dad. It's me. Sorry I'm so late. Can you come get me? I'm at the Ranger Station."

We could hear a drowsy voice answer, "That

you, Son? Where in heaven's name have you been? Do you know what time it is? We've been worried sick. Your mother even called the police. But they said they couldn't help, and that you were probably spending the night at a friend's house and forgot to tell us."

"Please, Dad, can you just come get me? I don't feel very well. I'm at the Ranger Station, off Castle Rock Road."

"Where's that?"

"Here, you can talk to the ranger."

Ron took the phone and gave the man directions. In about fifteen minutes an older model, diesel-powered, cream-colored BMW rattled up in front of the house. Father had arrived. He got out, wearing a white tee-shirt and crumpled pants, and trudged up to his son.

"Dammit, Son! How many times do we have to tell you? When you're going to be late, give us a call."

"I tried, Dad, honest, but the phone was busy."

"Oh, that must have been your younger sister. Since she turned eleven, the phone's become a permanent fixture in her ear."

"Please, Dad, can we just go? All I want to do is go to bed," touching his forehead like he had a headache.

"All right. But you haven't heard the last of this." The father started towards the car.

The kid quickly turned to Ron and whispered,

"Thanks. Ah, you're not going to tell my father what really happened, are you?"

Ron hesitated. "Well, I should make out a report, but since your. . . Oh, forget it. But I don't want to be awakened by you ever again, knockin' on my door at three in the mornin', or it's jail. You got that clear?" The kid gulped and climbed into the car. The time was 5 a.m.

The incident evidently made a lasting impression on the young man because several years later he brought his wife and his own two nice boys to the ranch and made a point of introducing them to Ranger Ron.

He said, "Remember me? I was the kid who ate the poisoned mushrooms and woke you up at three in the morning. I guess I did some pretty stupid things when I was a teenager."

Ron just smiled to himself.

What a Picnic

I remember one summer evening ten years after coming to the Borges Ranch. The kids and I, dressed and waiting patiently for Ron to get out of the shower, anticipated the annual neighborhood picnic at Castle Rock Park. Suddenly, the emergency bell outside our front door rang with a serious clarity. I answered the door.

A runner in shorts, sweat-stained tee-shirt and tennis shoes, and with his hair plastered to his head, gasped, "Down by the. . . pond. There's a horse. It's running free and acting crazy. I couldn't find the owner. He must have fallen off the horse on the trail somewhere. He may be hurt. Is the ranger here? Shouldn't someone call 911? Sorry, but I gotta go." He quickly dashed out of the yard and ran down the road, his duty done. Now it was up to the ranger.

I hurried down the hall to the bathroom to tell Ron what the runner had said. Ron was just stepping out of the shower. "Walk down to the picnic area to check things out while I get dressed," he said.

I swiftly walked over to the tack room, grabbed

a lead rope and halter, and hurried toward the picnic area. As I approached the site, I called out in a loud voice, "Is anyone there? Hello-o-o? Can anyone hear me?"

The only movement came from a large chestnut horse, about fifteen and a half hands—a man's horse, with its saddle on and reins hanging freely from its bit. It ran frantically on the lawn with flared nostrils, whinnying, snorting, kicking up divots of grass with its hooves, and throwing its head up and down as if ridding itself of an unwelcome hat on its head. Its neck, mane and forelock shone with soapy sweat. After a few minutes, it calmed down, walked around as if building up steam, then repeated the whole tantrum. I stayed clear, afraid I might spook the horse even more. I remembered Bill Hardy, our horseshoer, telling me once that he judged people like horses.

Again I yelled, "Hello? Can anyone hear me?" But no one answered.

The horse raised his head, shook his entire body and snorted. He then gave a kick with his hind legs in the air, and took off running across the field.

Ron came down the road in his truck and turned into the parking lot. He jumped out of his vehicle and yelled, "Don't worry about the horse, Marn. We can take care of him later. Right now, let's find the rider. Did the runner tell you which direction the horse came from?"

"No, he just said that there was a crazy horse

running around loose down by the pond, and a rider may be down somewhere."

"Maybe the rider's on the trail behind the dam. I'm going to drive up the fire road near there. Marn, I need you to stay here. I called 911, and a fire truck with paramedics should be here any minute."

After Ron left, I shouted again, but still no answer. Soon I heard a siren in the Castle Rock Road area, and the churning whine of truck wheels swerving fast up the ranch entry road. A red-and-gold-trimmed fire truck clattered over the cattle guard and stopped by the back gate of the parking lot. Two paramedics dressed in dark blue firemen's jackets with yellow stripes jumped out of the truck. I rushed up to them.

"I'm the ranger's wife. He called you because we believe there's a horseback rider down somewhere, and he may be hurt. His horse is over there." I pointed to the horse. It had finally calmed down and was nibbling the grass. "My husband drove up the fire trail in his truck looking for the rider. He should be back any minute."

About a half hour went by, and the paramedics started getting antsy. "Where did you say the ranger went?" one of them asked.

"He drove up that trail there, behind the dam." I pointed in the direction. "There's his truck now, coming down the hill." Ron was cautiously backing his vehicle down the hill on the fire road, because the road was too narrow to turn around.

He stopped when he got to the large gate, rolled down his window and shouted, "I think I saw something up a steep hill not far from here. It looked like an overstuffed black trash bag, or it may be a person on his side wedged against a barbed wire fence. You can follow me in your vehicle halfway up the fire road. But from there we'll have to hike up the hill, because it's too steep. Marn, I need you to stay here and wait for the ambulance and anyone else."

Ron put his truck in four-wheel drive and slowly crept back up the fire road. The fire truck followed. I could hear its gears grinding as it plodded up the hill, then just the sound of its engine idling.

About five minutes later, a red and white American Medical Response ambulance pulled into the parking lot and stopped near the back gate. Following close behind it was a black and white City of Walnut Creek police car. The officer recognized me and rolled down his window. "Everything okay?" he said. "I was in the area when I heard over the radio that someone on horseback may have gotten hurt."

"Yes. Ron and the paramedics are up on the hill right now, above the dam. Ron thinks he spotted the rider against a barbed wire fence. They should be down any minute."

The two ambulance men climbed out of their vehicle and went around to the back and opened its doors.

The police officer picked up his radio transmitter and spoke calmly into it: "Looks like they've got things under control here. I'll hang around for a few more minutes, just to make sure."

Soon a helicopter circled the area. It came in close with a deafening whirring sound. Then it dropped behind a hill and vanished. I could still hear the chopper's blades going around at a much fainter clip. After what seemed a long time, we saw the helicopter rise up from its hiding place like a swift, jerky hummingbird. It hovered for a moment then roared off in a beeline toward John Muir Hospital.

Ron and the fire truck backed slowly down the fire road. He opened the gate and drove into the parking lot with the fire truck following. His forehead was furrowed.

"It was a man, all right, pinned against the barbed wire fence way up on top of the hill," Ron said. "I got to him first, because I wasn't carrying any equipment. He was so still, I wasn't sure if he was dead or alive, but I performed CPR on him anyway, and he moaned.

"Apparently the man suffered a heart attack and fell off his horse, and rolled down the hill until the barbed wire fence stopped him. After the paramedics checked him over, we radioed for the helicopter to take him to John Muir Hospital, because he was in such bad shape. He may not make it." Ron sighed and shook his head. "If that runner hadn't come along when he did, the man probably wouldn't have had any chance at all. I'll call the hospital tomorrow and see how he is doing, and make out a report."

After the ambulance, police car and fire truck left, we finally caught the horse and put it in the corral for the night.

The next day, Ron phoned the hospital. He inquired about the man and obtained his identification, so he could contact a person to pick up the horse.

"Is he okay?" Ron inquired. His lower lip began quivering, and his eyes became watery. He hung up the phone. "Marn, the man died."

"Ron, you tried your best. What more could anyone ask?"

"Do you think his family will see it that way? I don't know how many times I've told people not to ride alone."

What a Feat

One day in the fall of 1986 Ron came in all excited after work.

"Hey, Marn, how would you like a new house?"

"You mean move from here? Did you get offered a better job?"

"No, there's this house that the city has to either tear down or move, over on Bishop Lane near the freeway, because it's sitting on the right-of-way for a new overpass. The city says it will cost more for tearing it down than moving it. They can move it for about $20,000. So Bob, my boss, suggested that they move it here for a new ranger house. It's in really good shape. Bob showed me around it today, and wanted me to show you. I think you'd like it. It's clean and modern. But we've got to act fast, if we want it. CalTrans needs it out of there in a couple of months. Come on, we'll go through the open space."

When we reached the new house, my face fell. It wasn't the type of house I was used to living in. It was about twenty years old, made of stucco with a synthetic shingled roof. A Spanish black wrought-iron grillwork encased the front porch.

Ron looked at me. "I know, I had the same reaction when I first saw it. But we can have all that ironwork taken off and put up our own posts." I smiled at his reassurance.

Ron lacked a key, so we walked around the house peeking in windows. It was dark inside because the walls had been painted a dark orange, which we both agreed must go. Traipsing around a yard that had not been manicured for some time and spying in windows, we figured out that there were three bedrooms, a kitchen, dining room, family room, living room, two bathrooms, and attached garage. Compared with our little house built in the 1930s it seemed a mansion. In the back yard we were surprised to find an empty Doughboy swimming pool full of decaying leaves, with a deck around it.

"Do the deck and pool come with the house?" I asked Ron.

"No. I already asked Bob. He said that the pool and decking are already spoken for by someone in the Parks Department. So are most of the plants. Besides, they won't let us have a pool at the ranch. They said it would be too much of a personal liability."

"Will our rent go up if we have a new house?"

"Ah, yeah, but I'm sure it won't be too much more."

I thought about the old house we'd lived in for the past eight years. We relished many memories of living in that house. Our two girls had grown up in it. Then I thought of its dark dining room with scuffed knotty-pine paneling, how we were always going down to the dark cellar, changing the glass fuses because our teenager used her hair dryer while I ironed. That twice the wall behind the bathtub had fallen out, how the faucets all leaked and kept us awake at night, how not a single window in the house shut tightly, and when you walked into the kitchen, the other end of the house would fly up. I could never keep the house clean, because dust continually crept under the door jambs. This new house with its modern conveniences, windows in every room and central air conditioning would propel us into the modern age. It even boasted a built-in dishwasher and microwave.

I looked at Ron. "When would they move it to the ranch?"

"The city's already contracted with Troust Brothers to move it. They're just waiting for our okay. You know that flagship of Howard Hughes out in Suisun Bay called the 'Glomar Explorer' that I pointed out to you. Well, Troust Brothers were the only ones who could move it, so they must be pretty good. They plan to jack the house up and transport it through the open space in two sections on a big flatbed swivel trailer. They said they might have to remove a few trees, but it won't be bad. But first they'll tear down our old house and build a new foundation.

"While they're doing that," he continued,

"they'll bring in a trailer for us to live in. They want all this done before the winter rains come in late November, so we should be in our new house just before Christmas. What do you think?"

"All right. If you're happy, I'm happy."

The next couple of weeks produced a whirlwind. A trailer arrived for us to live in. But it was a contractor's mobile office with two sliding windows in front and two entry doors on either side. It included one small window on one of the sides, and none in the back. One large room in the front had a counter, and two small office-size rooms in the back were supposed to serve as bedrooms. Our so-called kitchen consisted of the counter and, over to one side, a sunken stainless steel sink, hot plate and portable refrigerator underneath that required a hands-and-knees approach for access. It resembled a mini bar more than a kitchen.

The trailer's bathroom was even smaller than our closet-sized one in the old house, but it did include a functioning toilet, sink, and small shower, but no electrical outlets. They backed the office trailer up near the blacksmith shop, then ran a hose for water from the nearby spigot, attached an extension cord for our electricity, and stuffed a long black flexible connecting tube into one end of our old septic tank.

We were told to move into the trailer only our beds, couch and a card table with chairs. Our queen-size bed just barely fit in one of the small office rooms, with no room for a bureau drawer. Lacking closets, we hung our clothes on hooks screwed into the walls, and kept the rest of our personal belongings in cardboard boxes.

In the other small office, Ron put a strip of masking tape down the middle of the room between the girls' single beds and told them to make do or else. We stored our less immediate household items and furniture in various outbuildings around the ranch.

Kristin, our oldest, now a senior in high school, thought it was an extreme sacrifice, sharing a cramped room with her eleven-year-old sister, and complained that Kim's stuff would be all over her side of the room. In actuality it was the other way around. Kristin's stuff flowed over to Kim's side of the room and it was Kim who complained. Their battles on occasion really frayed our nerves.

We were told that we could strip the old house of any fixtures or materials that we deemed salvageable. Ron spent a week ripping knotty-pine paneling off the walls and storing it in the shed by the blacksmith shop.

Then one day, James Farr, the contractor, brought in a bulldozer whose powerful jaws crunched down our little old house into its cellar within minutes. The entire house splintered, then with a slight puff of dust, neatly devoured itself. They pushed dirt on top of the hole and leveled it off.

Adjacent to the burial ground, they built a new foundation, matching the floor plan of the house coming our way. They also put in plumbing and electrical pipes exactly as they were laid out in the new house, and a concrete wall about two and a half feet high that the house would sit on. How they duplicated the exact measurements was beyond me.

The foundation was soon complete, and we awaited the big move. Then that night it started raining, and it rained, and it rained. The project came to a halt. A river of mud from the excavation site, rocks, debris, including garbage bags, shingles, branches, and old tar paper swept down the entry road right underneath the trailer. We felt like we were on Noah's Ark watching the last remains of our world go by.

We spent Christmas Eve huddled around a spindly miniature Christmas tree perched on the countertop, sipping cups of instant hot chocolate and hoping it would stop raining. But it continued raining right through January and February on into March.

Then one day the rain stopped. A couple of weeks went by and the waters dried up. The green hills attracted people and animals who once again walked on the trails. It was time to make the big move.

The new house, separated from the garage, perched on jacks. We were told that it would be brought over in two sections. Ron Troust put his big red rig in gear and slowly backed the flatbed trailer underneath the house a few feet at a time. As they moved, his crew skillfully discarded the blocks and jacks that lifted the house until they had it entirely balanced on the bed. He was an artist, to say the least.

A couple of days beforehand, the newspaper publicized the move. On the big day, it looked like an old-time circus parade. Adults, children and photographers lined the roadway along Bishop Lane, Rudgear Road and Walnut Boulevard. People even climbed on rooftops for a glimpse of the ranger's house going by. As a starting signal for the long-awaited journey of the house to its new Borges Ranch location, Troust pulled on his loud diesel truck horn with an eardrum-bursting blast.

The double-wide gates at the end of Walnut Boulevard near Rocksprings swung open, welcoming the procession into the open space. The huge rig and tractor groaned and creaked as it strained inch by inch up the steep grade toward Mt. Diablo Trail—the toughest part of the journey. Troust's son rode in the flag truck ahead of the big rig, and Ron's truck led the way. At one section the trail narrowed so much they held their breaths as one set of tires hung momentarily in the air. Slowly the truck and its precious cargo snaked its way up and down the trail through the hills. It curved around sloping hills like a freight train traveling through the mountains. Sadly, a large oak tree toppled over as the large truck and tractor sideswiped it. The roots held, but the tree still lies on its side as a reminder of that unforgettable day.

On the last leg of the journey the vehicles encountered a hairpin turn leading down the back trail to the ranch complex. On the first attempt, the tractor and rig were almost bent in half; chains and sway bars nearly jackknifed and buckled. Troust pumped the brakes to slow the rig. A smell of burnt rubber and diesel permeated the air as the truck slowed and skidded to a halt on the loose gravel and dirt. After a moment of silence Troust climbed down from the cab and surveyed the situation. He called to his crew, "Don't know if we can make it, fellas. She's pretty tight."

Ron, puzzled about the holdup, hiked back up the trail and joined Troust. "I thought we could make it, Ron, but she's just too darn wide to make the swing."

"What if you backed her up a little and made a wide turn onto the parallel road that leads down into the corral? From there, I could cut a swipe with my D-4 Cat across to the main trail that leads down to the ranch."

Troust pulled a red kerchief out of his back pocket, took off his cap and wiped the sweat from his forehead. "You know, it might work. But we'll have to take her easy 'cause of the soft ground."

On Troust's okay, Ron fired up the 1937 D-4

Caterpillar and crawled up the hill. He made several swipes back and forth, making a connecting trail with the original. Troust looked at the span.

"She'll do!" he shouted. A big cheer went up from everyone. Troust then signaled his crew to put things back in motion. He slowly backed the truck and tractor, made a wide swing onto the corral trail, then cautiously crept across the newly created span of trail. Only for a second did the wheels spin in the soft dirt, but the rig kept going. Once he reached the old trail, there was no stopping him. The truck and house gracefully slid down the hill, through the large cattle gate and halted within a few feet of the new foundation. Troust got out and looked it over. He carefully backed up the rig and tractor onto the foundation, as if he did that sort of thing every day. As he inched forward, the house gradually settled onto its new resting place. Another cheer went up and echoed through the hills.

George Barber

RANGER Ron checks what's coming from behind.

Brian Murphy

WESTERN Diamondback Rattlesnake measures from 3-7 feet and likes dry grasslands, brushy areas and rocky foothills. Diamonds often are faded or spotty.

Rattlesnake

It was 9 p.m., after a long day. The campers were settled at Hanna Grove for the night, and Ron finally relaxed on the family room sofa with a beer and began watching the last quarter of the 49er football game.

Just as he settled back, our two dogs, Jake and Amber, started barking furiously. At first, Ron ignored the din because Amber barked at anything that walked by. He thought it was just a camper walking around the ranch. Then he heard a loud hissing sound like a water pipe had burst.

Annoyed by the disturbance, Ron got up, opened the back door without turning on the porch light, and looked out into a black void. He couldn't see anything, but he could hear a terrific hissing sound. He bent over, wondering if a water pipe had sprung a leak next to the house. Suddenly, something struck him hard, and a sharp, piercing pain shot through his right hand.

"Jeez! It's a rattlesnake! And it bit me!" he shouted.

"What? A snake bit you? Where?"

"On my hand, and it was a big one. I didn't even

see it coming."

I rushed to the door, turned the porch light on, and opened the door a crack. Ron was hurrying down the walkway toward the tool shed.

"Ron! Ron! Where are you going? We've got to get you to a hospital right away."

"No! First I've got to get a shovel and kill the thing before it bites someone else. Call the dogs in and see if it bit one of them."

As soon as I opened the door , the two of them scrambled inside. Our two-year-old Jake sidled up to me and didn't leave my side. Amber, our fourteen-year-old shepherd, lay down under the coffee table. I checked them over but didn't find any bites. I then rushed out the front door after Ron. He was fast making his way back toward the porch with a flat, sharp-edged shovel in his hand. "Get in the house and stay there! I don't want you bitten too," he yelled.

"But, but you might get bitten again if you try to kill it."

"I have to kill it or nobody will believe me," he retorted.

From the window in the back door, I watched Ron swiftly hack the snake in two with the sharp edge of the shovel, just below its diamond-shaped head. Even with its head cut off, the snake's body continued wiggling and squirming, and its jaw gaped open and shut. Then the snake lay still. When satisfied it was truly dead, I opened the door and calmly tapped Ron on the shoulder. He leaned the shovel against the house and staggered back, spent of his adrenaline.

"Okay, now we can go to the hospital," he said. I took him into the kitchen, grabbed some ice from the freezer and stuffed it into a plastic bag. He held it against his swelling hand. "Keep your hand and arm above your head," I said. Together we walked to the car.

Ron sat by me as I drove through the open space over the fire roads to Kaiser Hospital in Walnut Creek. Just before we reached the Rockspring gate, we saw a father, mother and young girl out walking in the open space in the dark. I rolled down the window and nervously yelled at them, "The park's closed at night. Please go home. It's dangerous. My husband was just bitten by a rattlesnake." It was the wrong thing to say, but it was the first thing that came to mind.

The girl started screaming and clinging to her father. He yelled at her, "Stop that, Amanda!" As if on cue, she stopped screaming and looked up at him.

"Is he all right?" he asked.

"I don't know. We're on our way to the hospital right now. Please go home. You're not supposed to be in the open space after dark."

The girl looked up at her father, then started screaming again. Before I could stop Ron, he jumped out of the car and opened the gate. I quickly drove through, and he closed the gate behind us and got back in the car. As we neared the hospital, Ron said he felt light-headed with some numbness in his face and chin. I looked at his face. It was ashen.

"You better hurry, Marn. I don't feel so good." I put my flasher lights on and drove as fast as I dared on the back streets. At the first red light, Ron turned to me and said, "Go!"

"But I'm scared, Ron. What if I hit someone?"

"Just go! Don't worry about it."

"Don't worry about it? Okay!"

I swallowed hard, then leaned on the horn and ran two red lights. After what felt like an eternity, I pulled into the Kaiser parking lot. Ron stepped out and headed into the emergency ward. The parking attendant said he would park the car.

I doggedly followed after Ron. When he announced at the reception desk that he'd been bitten by a rattlesnake, nurses immediately ushered him into emergency, where they sat him down and took his temperature and blood pressure. Then a nurse pumped him for information. How long ago was it that the snake bit you? Are you sure it was a rattlesnake? Did you see it? Are you allergic to any drugs? Was it an on-the-job injury? Were you drinking?

Both Ron and I became exasperated by the flood of inane questions. "Yes, I'm sure it was a rattlesnake," he snapped. "Yes, I saw it. I even

143

killed it. Do you want my wife to go get it, so I can prove to you it really was a snake?"

After Ron thoroughly convinced the nurse and several other hospital staff members of the event, they took him into an exam room where a nurse helped him remove his shirt and had him lie down on a gurney. His hand started swelling even more, and he complained about a "numbness and pins-and-needles tingling, like when your leg falls asleep. And there's a burning sensation traveling from my lower face, down the shoulders, chest, arms, groin area and legs," he said. A doctor finally came in and asked Ron another battery of questions, examined the puncture wounds on his hand, then left to call Poison Control Center.

I sat alone in the room with Ron. He started shaking and felt clammy. I suspected he might go into shock or pass out, so I kept talking to him. The nurse came in and attached an intravenous needle to Ron's left wrist, started an IV and put a blanket over him. About a half hour later the doctor came back, looked at Ron's hand again and instructed the nurse to start anti-venom. The nurse hooked up the first bag through a second needle attached to the first one.

"It looks like you'll be spending the night with us," she told Ron. "And Mrs. White, you should go home." She gave me a number to call the next day to find out which room he would be in.

I kissed my dear Ron good-bye, and he forced

a smile and whispered, "Don't worry. I'll be okay. Save the snake, if you can. I want to make a hat band out of it."

Back at the ranch, I locked the gate, turned out the lights and put the dogs in the garage for the night. Normally they slept on the porch and didn't like being shut up in the garage, but that night they seemed content.

I looked through the window at the dead snake several times before going outside. I finally convinced myself that it couldn't come alive and slither away. The blood around it had dried and looked frozen, but ants already feasted on it. I selected my large aluminum salad bowl, opened the back door, took the shovel Ron had killed it with, and bravely moved in closer. Goose bumps the size of lemons popped up on my arms and back. "It's dead," I kept telling myself. "You fool. You've nothing to be afraid of."

I squeezed my eyes shut a moment, took a deep breath, gingerly slid the shovel under the snake and scooped it up into the bowl like it was a huge "dog doo." Under the porch light, I took a good look. It wasn't like the long brown and tan ones I had seen when we lived on the desert. Their diamonds are more distinguishable, like their imitator, the gopher snake. Instead, it was about a foot and a half long, dark gray with lighter gray diamonds on its back, quite thick, with a flat diamond-shaped head, black beady eyes and a black forked tongue. It had eight rattles or buttons that graduated to a point and looked like a wheat head.

I leaned the shovel up against the house, picked up the bowl and hurriedly locked it up in the large storage refrigerator in the garage. As I entered the garage, Jake ran up to me and jumped at the bowl. He must have smelled the snake. Later I learned rattlesnakes give off an offensive odor like fresh-cut cucumbers. But I didn't smell anything. Even though I knew the snake was dead, I feared that I might drop the bowl and it would somehow come alive again.

I trembled. Snakes weren't the only predators invading our area. Because of an overpopulation of ground squirrels and mice, and severe drought conditions, coyotes were a common sight at all times of the day in the open space. I spotted one just the day before on the hill above the ranch, while talking with Dan Borges. Some coyotes are bold, territorial and protective of their young. Several sightings of eagles, bobcats and hawks also kept me alert.

After waking up Saturday morning, I checked the refrigerator just in case the snake had slithered away in the night, and that it wasn't just a dream. I took a good look. It was still there, all right. I slammed the refrigerator door shut.

I dressed, fed the farm animals, made sure the campers had cleaned up the site, and talked to a new group of people with a Hanna Grove reservation for a family reunion. I told them Ron was sick, and asked if they would bag their own garbage. I didn't want to advertise the exact nature of his illness.

In the afternoon, I visited Ron at the hospital. I brought him a shiny vinyl balloon with Mickey and Minnie Mouse on it saying, "You're Special," and a bag of Jelly Bellies.

"How are you feeling?" I asked.

"My hand hurts, my head aches, and I'm tired because the nurses kept waking me every hour during the night, checking on me. And the doctor says he wants me to spend another night."

I stayed only an hour and told him to rest. When I returned in the evening Ron said he felt a little better, and not a jelly bean remained.

That night back at the ranch, the Mexican Fiesta was in full swing. About 150 people were drinking beer, barbecuing, and dancing to Mexican guitar music reverberating all the way over the open space to Northgate Road, blocks away. At 10:30 p.m. the police called, saying they'd received a complaint of loud music coming from the Borges Ranch. Not wanting the police storming the ranch and busting things up, I told them that I'd take care of it. After all, it was a family reunion. At 10:45 p.m. I jumped in the station wagon and drove down to the Hanna Grove picnic site. I asked several half-looped people the whereabouts of the gentleman in charge. He, too, appeared wobbly, but obligingly said they'd quit the music. I gave him fifteen minutes to wrap it up.

On Sunday morning, Ron called me to pick him up at the hospital. I was late, because I still had to feed the farm animals. When I got there, he was dressed and sitting on the bed. He said he had walked over to the pharmacy to get his pills. "You better take it easy," I said.

In the car on the way home, I tried joking about the snake, and what Ron's boss would say, but my recuperating ranger husband wasn't too talkative. As we neared home, he insisted that we stop at the picnic area. He made sure the site was cleaned up properly, liners put in the garbage cans and toilet paper in the outhouses, because a wedding was scheduled that afternoon.

I told Ron not to worry about it, but he's conscientious and sometimes can be stubborn, and he insisted on checking everything anyway.

After fifteen minutes Ron came back to the car looking peaked. I drove him to the house where he lay down on the couch. Within ten minutes he began snoring and slept through the night until 9 a.m.

He lounged around Monday and Tuesday, then on Wednesday insisted on going back to work, even though his head still ached and his stomach bothered him. For the rest of the week Ron worked light duty, still feeling the effects of the bite and medicine as late as Friday. I kept gritting my teeth, as he was really grouchy and impatient. He hates being sick. I rejoiced when Monday rolled around and he felt ready for full-time work.

For quite a while, we didn't see any more rattlesnakes. Then one day Ron radioed me, "I'm going to be late coming in, Marn. Would you turn on the hot water for the calves' suckle in the barn? I'll feed them when I get back."

After turning on the electric water heater, I checked on the calves back of the barn in the field. All three black and white Holstein calves saw me and came charging down the hill toward me, their skinny rag-tipped tails flying in the wind. I petted each one of them and threw a flake of alfalfa into their feeder, which they quickly noticed. I walked back through the barn and left the back door ajar so they could push it open and go inside if the weather turned windy and cold. I closed and latched the front barn door behind me and went into the house.

Later, I heard Ron's truck pull into the drive, and instead of stopping at the house, he went directly to the barn to give the calves their suckle. A half hour later Ron came in the house wide-eyed.

"Marn, did you open the back door to the barn and leave it ajar?"

"Yes, Ron, so the calves could come in the barn on their own if it got cold."

"I guess you didn't see the snake," he said excitedly.

"Snake? What snake? Where?" I retorted.

"When I went through the back door to bring in

the calves, I noticed a shiny black-forked tongue darting in and out. It belonged to a snake lying along the ledge right next to the piece of wood that keeps the door shut. It was another rattlesnake, about two feet long. It had ten rattles. You know, Marn, if you had made any sudden movement or noise, that snake could have bitten you right on the cheek. It had to be no more than six inches away from you."

"Oh, my God! Did you kill it?"

"Yes. And I threw its stinkin' body over the corral fence into the manure pile."

ANOTHER open area predator, the bobcat also likes chaparral, oak woodlands and the forest. Its head and body measures from 26 to 36 inches plus a 5 inch tail.

A New Visitor Center

Even with the protection of the National Register, the restoration of the original Borges family home still remained an issue. The deteriorated old house, as the years went by, looked sadder and sadder with sunken dark eyes, like a wizened old man with an incurable disease. In my heart, I wanted to help give the old building back its dignity and life. After serving the Borges family well for five generations, it deserved a role as the cornerstone of the ranch. Children and adult visitors paid rapt attention when learning about its structure and history.

But many people, including city engineers, scoffed at the idea of restoring it. In their opinion the best step was to tear it down. But we had one ace in the hole: Its National Register of Historic Places listing required special permission from the State of California Office of Historic Preservation for any changes.

It was 1988. One day while scanning the newspaper, I read an article about grants being offered by the Office of Historic Preservation in Sacramento for restoration of historic buildings on the

National Register. I showed Bob Pond the article. His words, "Let's go for it," sounded familiar.

We applied and felt lucky to receive a $78,000 grant. There was one catch, however. The restoration had to be completed within a certain time frame, or we would lose the grant.

The city received initial bids from contractors desiring the work, but at a price well above $78,000. In the meantime, Bob, diagnosed with leukemia, became quite ill. Ron took over the bulk of open space duties, and the restoration project ended up on the back burner. Bob continued working when he could as a consultant, but nearly a year had elapsed.

Then one day a letter arrived from the Office of Historic Preservation warning us that unless we started restoration on the old house soon, we would lose the grant. As a last-ditch effort to come up with the extra needed funds, Bob persuaded the city to use contingency money from the original Public Land Dedication Fund. The city granted his request. I will always be grateful to Bob for his efforts, because it was the last major thing he did before his death in 1990.

Bob's letter to the State Office of Historic Preservation pleaded for an extension and said that we possessed the extra needed funds. Someone in that office evidently felt sorry for us or shared the same dream of seeing the house completed, because, to our jubilation, the grant was extended.

Frank Bryant, a local contractor, said he could do the work within our budget, and restoration started immediately. His crew first raised the building off the ground, so a new foundation could be constructed. Workers jacked the house up and put the delicate framework precariously on blocks. One evening at 5:05 in 1989, the San Francisco Bay Area began shaking, including the old ranch house. The major quake lasted about two and a half minutes, with several aftershocks. Bridges and freeways collapsed and buildings tumbled.

We rushed outside expecting to see a pile of rubble, but the house seemed determined to stand its ground. After that, there was no stopping us. We took it as a sign that the house itself was anxious to be rebuilt.

Soon a new foundation took shape. Individuals and volunteers worked alongside the contractors, helping dismantle the walls and flooring, thus speeding things along.

After removing the first wall, we discovered that the house was a prefab and the walls were in sections, so the job became simpler than anticipated. Wall studs were actual two-by-fours located every six feet, instead of every four feet required by today's building code. The windows and door jambs were all individual sizes, and new ones had to be specially made. When the workers removed the few remaining shingles from the roof they were surprised to find the original builders had used actual two-by-four support beams instead of today's standard four-by-six. A heavy person taking a walk on the roof could have fallen in.

One day a worker was taking down some of the siding near the top of the roof and the whole wall came tumbling down like dominoes, with him skiing down on top of it. He wasn't hurt, but the incident required extra costs in materials and time, neither of which we could afford.

The sections of tongue-in-groove walls and flooring were carefully numbered and placed in piles to be put back exactly where they had been taken down. Before putting the walls back up, we hired an electrician who installed new wiring in the house. A new floor was made for the kitchen and hallway, but the parlor and bedroom floors were left intact with the exception of a few boards that had to be reversed or replaced. While doing the floors, we discovered there were three layers of flooring in the old house. When one layer wore out, the family simply put another layer over the top, and raised the baseboards. It didn't matter height-wise, because of the fourteen-foot ceilings.

The work went fairly smoothly, and by late summer the house was nearly completed. After restoring the outside structure, the workers brought back the natural color of the redwood through a special bleaching process.

Once the process was completed, the wood looked fresh and new. We asked the contractors what the plans called for painting the interior walls. We were told they were going to be painted an aqua blue with orange baseboards, door jambs and window frames. Our reaction was "Yuck!"

Ron and I immediately protested. The original colors of the house had been off-white with a dark Japanese green trim. Fortunately, we called the painting contractor before he ordered the paint. He said they would paint the walls an off-white, only because it was standard paint and cheaper, but we would have to pick our own color for the trim at our expense. Ron and I decided that the original Japanese green was too dark, so we requested a softer, more pleasing green. We asked the workers not to paint the new sections of redwood, only to stain them a natural shade that enhanced the richness of the wood in contrast with the off-white walls.

The effect was beautiful. But time was running short. We imagined naturally varnished floors, but the workers argued that it wasn't in the plans and time and money were gone. One day after work, I came home to find the floors had been hurriedly painted a mousy brown. The workers didn't even sand or hammer back in the old nails. With the final touch-up to the window jambs, they said their work on the house was completed.

Slightly disappointed, we thanked them for a job well done. Sort of kiddingly, they told us that in spite of a few cogs in the wheel, meaning our preference in paint, the work had gone fairly well, and they enjoyed doing it. It gave them satisfaction to bring new life to an old building again, they said. Whenever they entered the house, they experienced a good feeling, like the house really appreciated their efforts, they said. They also found no cold or eerie spots, which sometimes chill old houses.

Students from the high school, scouts, church groups and friends lent a hand on the last finishing touches such as picking up scrap, painting trim, constructing window boxes for flowers, and helping Dan Borges landscape and lay the rock walls.

As the crowning finish, the Borges family held a reunion at the ranch and put up the blocks containing their memorabilia under the porch in the front of the house. They also installed a plaque honoring the Borges Ranch house. During the house restoration, the City Council was offering Civic Pride Grants. I filled out the necessary paperwork, obtained letters of support from various agencies and prestigious individuals within our community, and nervously spoke before the council requesting a grant for displays in the new Visitor Center or old house. To my surprise, the council members granted the Walnut Creek Open Space Foundation $22,000, plus $10,000 in matching money from the foundation's funds to furnish the home.

We hired a local retired carpenter who built display cabinets and installed a decorative fire wall

behind a 1904 Pride stove, which we had pur-
chased to heat the house. With the help of a local
artist we worked long hours on designing for the
display cabinets. We wanted a subtle flavor of the
late 1800s era, without drawing attention away
from the house itself. We wanted a feeling of cozi-
ness, like you'd feel visiting your grandma's house.

On our days off, Ron and I scrounged at flea
markets and antique shops for needed display
items, such as glass knobs for the doors, copper
door plates, authentic period furnishings, and mod-
est chandeliers. We went as far north as Ferndale,
California, purchasing a 1903 cast-iron chrome-
plated Stewart stove for the kitchen, and a freestanding kitchen cabinet. We also acquired through
donations various antique labor-saving devices,
such as an apple corer, cherry pitter, meat grinder,
bread crumb maker, bread kneader, juicer, pea
sheller, Universal cake maker, Wagner waffle iron
and a collection of sad and flat irons.

Friends donated a 1902 Sears Roebuck tin bathtub, a rocker, antique clothes washer, kerosene
lamps, rag rugs, straight razors and musical instru-
ments. One woman sewed the curtains and
valances for the windows, and a man fixed up the
plumbing in the bathroom so that the 1880s P.T.
Crapper model toilet actually flushed and
swooshed.

We stayed up late at night doing research and
text work, painting baseboards, and setting up dis-

plays. We wanted to show the city we could do a super job for the least amount of money. I even wrote a script for the old-fashioned crank telephone, and together with Ron's mom, recorded an authentic sounding 1906 conversation about the earthquake in San Francisco. Ron's stepfather rigged up the recording system.

On opening day, we held a special catered party for city employees and contributors to the house. The historic house became an instant success and focal point of the ranch.

Unfortunately, Bob Pond, the open space specialist and Ron's first boss, didn't live to see the finished product. In his memory, a small plaque was placed in a corner of the parlor with the engraved inscription, "Bob Pond Room."

Ranger Ron Slays a Wild Boar

The first rains doused us in early November about the same day the Contra Costa Times printed an article about a wild pig rooting up a man's lawn in Orinda. We thought it funny until we heard rumors of feral pigs causing damage on Mt. Diablo. Then, after one of our neighbors sighted a loose black pig near the Borges Ranch, the Walnut Creek Open Space employees decided they'd take matters into their own hands.

They issued a notice asking people to notify the rangers and maintenance workers if they saw any further evidence of pigs' existence on Shell Ridge. As a deterrent, we left lights on overnight at the Hanna Grove Picnic Site and at the Borges Ranch.

Within a couple of days, a pig visited the Hanna Grove picnic area during the night, leaving several telltale furrows in the middle of the lawn. Two days later a pig churned up dirt around some of the antique farm equipment at the ranch.

My husband, Ranger Ron, fearing similar damage to the expensive sod lawn recently planted in front of the new visitor center, concocted the idea of connecting an infrared light sensor to the gate leading to the animal area. In addition, he attached a wire with a buzzer in our bedroom, set to go off when the sensor was activated. He also rigged up a long rope from the house to the animal area gate. When he jerked the rope it closed the gate, thus trapping any visitor. Ron baited the area leading to the gate with food as a lure.

The trick worked. At 2:30 one morning, the alarm sounded—as did every rooster on the ranch. Ron woke with a start, pulled on the rope, and heard the clanking of the gate as it slammed shut, trapping the intruder. Ron jumped out of bed and looked out the bedroom window at the dark shadow of a large pig nosing its way across the yard. He hurriedly put on his pants, shirt and shoes, grabbed the 12-gauge shotgun, loaded it with solid slugs, and headed out the door to his truck, which he had parked near the fence.

Ron positioned the truck spotlight on the animal area. The pig, blinded by the intense light, took off at a run. Ranger Ron took careful aim and fired a slug into the pig's heart. It didn't even faze the pig, and it charged toward the fence in the direction of the parked vehicle, where it finally dropped.

The only sound in the entire barnyard was the swishing sound of blood gushing out of the animal's wound. When Ron reached the pig, it was still struggling to get up. Not wanting the boar to suffer any longer, Ron finished it off with a slug in the side of the head near the ear, which is the humane and quickest way of disposing of a pig.

Ron didn't want to waste the meat, so he threw a rope over a limb of a tree, strung the carcass up, and field dressed it on the spot. It was cold enough that the meat would not spoil by morning. He then went back to bed.

In the morning, the thought of seeing the pig didn't thrill me, especially on an empty stomach, but not wanting to disappoint Ron, I trudged toward the windmill where he'd strung it up. "It weighed in at nearly three hundred pounds," Ron said with a trace of pride.

There dangled the ugliest, meanest looking pig I'd ever seen. Its long black body was heavily coated with bristles. It had an elongated snout for rooting, long legs, large ears and, even in death, piercing, menacing black eyes. A pair of four-inch-long yellowish tusks stuck out both sides of its jaw, and a row of vicious looking, sharp teeth protruded from the gaping mouth. Ron had gutted it, and the chest and stomach cavity exposed bright red ribs. He told me to hold the pig steady while he took a photo of it. I nearly puked.

Ron dislikes hunting or the killing of a wild animal, but this time he had a good excuse to use a gun. The wild pigs represented a threat to the safety of the public and the open space environment.

Morning after First Rainfall
By Marnie White

Rain water streaming down orange-streaked
rusty tin barn roof
digging whiskey-colored trenches in sandy
soil unfurling curled dusty fists
of gray apple leaves

Fresh aroma of damp dirt filling my nostrils
reminding me of my grandmother kneeling
in her garden planting tulip bulbs
her brown-weathered hands patting
the moist earth

* * * * *

The Barn Also Gets a Face Lift

With the old house restored, the Borges Ranch appeared complete. But it still lacked one more thing to make it special—a protected place where students and groups could spend the night during inclement weather, and a place that also served for meetings and parties. The horse barn built by Francisco Borges in 1903 would be the ideal building.

The following year, I again applied for a Civic Pride Grant, this time for $5,000, with a promise of matching funds. At the hearing, a new council member, Ron Beagley, kiddingly asked me if this would be the last grant we would ever ask for. I hesitated, then told him I hoped so but couldn't be certain. He just smiled and the grant was ours.

That fall, I hired Dan Borges and Bill Hardy. "Put a new foundation under the barn and do whatever else you feel is necessary to make it functional," I said. Because his grandfather, Frank Borges, built the barn, Dan took special pride in handling the project and did much more than was expected of him.

To begin with, I helped Dan take various measurements that he jotted down on a piece of scrap paper. He handed me a list of needed materials, which I ordered from the local lumber yard. He didn't draw any specific plans; he carried in his head the construction and building skills he'd learned from his father. More than a week passed before the lumber and other materials arrived.

In the meantime, we shoveled out nearly four feet of accumulated dried cow and horse manure and rotting straw, surveyed the site, and brought in dirt and gravel to level the slope and grade the ground. Dan and Bill then placed various stakes at precise locations and strung a grid of string lines. At each cross section they placed a cement base, making sure it was level.

To these they screwed and nailed four-by-six beams and joists. On top of the beams they nailed flooring made up of two-by-twelve rough cut redwood planks covering the entire area of the barn. At the far end of the barn, they built a wall of one-by-twelve rough cut boards that reached the ceiling. They put in a handicap ramp with a sliding door and a long bench under the open window in the back of the barn for guests, and trimmed the existing support posts.

It was now mid-March, and the weather turned so cold our hands hurt and we could barely work. My father had given Ron an old wood-burning stove for his shop, which he never installed. I suggested setting it up in the barn temporarily to keep us warm, but Dan and Bill thought of another idea.

As long as they were installing a stove, why not make it permanent? The grant didn't stipulate specific changes, just to improve the barn as a classroom and meeting place.

So, they first built a box on the floor in which they put bricks as a pad for the stove. I helped by grouting the bricks with sand. They placed a fire wall behind the stove. We bought new stovepipes, a hood for the tin barn roof, and caulking material. The stove became a wonderful asset and still warms the backside of many a grateful visitor to the ranch.

One day while working in the barn, the new open space superintendent, Dan Cather, dropped in. He seemed pleased with our progress, and I introduced him to Dan Borges and Bill Hardy.

My budget included funds for hiring a carpenter to make three large display cabinets out of the same rough redwood boards. A good friend skilled in designing and photography offered his assistance in laying out the displays for the three cabinets. On the newly constructed wall we designed a pattern of old-time farm equipment collected over the years. I showed the superintendent the tool display on the wall, and he seemed pleased.

For a festive look, we hung colorful quilts and Navajo blankets on the walls. On the first weekend in June, we completed the barn just in time for our annual Borges Ranch Day Celebration and the Statewide Mayors Conference.

On the day of the Mayors Conference, after giving a tour to first graders, I told them a lot of mayors would be in the barn later. A child spoke up, "You're going to let horses in here?"

That evening, I told the mayors what the boy had said, and they took it in good stride. Some laughed out loud. They marveled at what we'd accomplished for so little money. "The money only paid for the materials," I said. "The true restoration came from love of the ranch."

With the old house restored and the barn renovated, our educational programs increased so much that the Walnut Creek Open Space Foundation directors experienced difficulty in handling all the financial responsibilities along with their own interests. They felt the Borges Ranch interpretive programs should become a separate entity.

I knew it was coming. The new open space superintendent called me into his office and said that the foundation no longer wanted the responsibility of overseeing the Borges Ranch educational programs. It didn't surprise me because of foundation board member hints the past year. Letting go of the foundation was hard, though, because I'd started it. It originally had been my baby. I think the superintendent expected me to react differently, but I just said, "Okay, then we'll start another nonprofit organization."

I completed the paperwork within a few months. We named it the Borges Ranch Interpretive Association. Nearly eight months passed before our final determination letters arrived from both the state and federal agencies.

Today, the Borges Ranch Interpretive Association operates as capably and successfully as the Walnut Creek Open Space Foundation. Its purpose: to provide educational programs, assist with special events and open space projects, and preserve and protect the open space environment. As a result, the City of Walnut Creek Open Space now boasts two supporting agencies and another feather in its hat.

Fifties Bull

It was a sad day. The huge double-decker cattle truck rumbled over the cattle guard into the yard and backed up to the loading chute. In the corral, Dan Borges' entire herd of red and white Herefords and Black Angus cattle, which he'd rounded up the day before, milled around. Dan was in a terrible, sour mood. He kept taking deep breaths and letting them out. You could taste and smell the tension that lingered in the air. It caused an acrid smell, and left a nasty bitter bite.

California's severe drought kept the grass low and the price of cattle at rock bottom. Ron had the "dirty duty" of telling Dan Borges to remove most of his cattle from the open space land. This really upset Dan, because he had no place for the herd and would be forced to sell them at a loss. Ron told Dan that he could hang onto a small number of his cows and calves, but with Dan it was all or nothing.

The ranch had been in his family for seventy-five years, and now a snot-nosed, uppity kid of a ranger, whom he'd taught almost everything he knew about ranching—from fixing fences to building barns—was double-crossing him by telling him,

"Sell your cattle and get out." Dan was stubborn in his Portuguese way, and so was Ron, because his job was on the line. They were two bulls butting heads.

Ron felt bad, because it seemed like telling his own father, "Give up everything you own and move into a retirement home." We respected Dan and loved him.

I watched as the first cows clambered into the truck. The clatter of their hooves going up the ramp hurt my ears. I didn't want to hear or see any more, so I went about my chores of feeding the farm animals.

In about an hour, most of the cattle, including Dan's prize bull, Ferdinand, had been loaded. Only a few cows and calves remained in the corral. I braved the tension and went up to him. "Dan, I'm sorry you have to get rid of your cattle, but it was out of our hands. I wish you'd change your mind and keep at least some of the cows and calves."

Dan just clenched his mouth shut and ignored my pleading. He went over to a cow and her calf and picked up the two-day-old Hereford. He shoved the calf into my arms. Surprised, I almost dropped it. It weighed almost forty pounds.

"Here, you want 'em so bad, you take care of 'em," he growled. The workers loaded the rest of the cattle, including the calf's mother, into the truck. Dan and the crew drove off, leaving me with the orphan amid a mysterious calm that suddenly blanketed the ranch.

I took the calf over to the other barn, away from the previous turmoil, and spread some fresh straw on the barn floor. He toddled over to me, bawled, and rubbed his downy-white head against my thigh. He took a corner of my shirt in his mouth and began sucking. I pulled it away from him and laughed.

"Hey, stop that."

I still owned an old pail with a nipple that helped me raise three other orphaned calves. But I needed some suckle from the feed store. The baby's pink, white and wet nose felt cold against my hand. Dan said the baby had been born only two days earlier. I noted the date. The remains of his umbilical cord still dangled from his abdomen, and he wasn't castrated.

An idea began brewing in the back of my mind. Maybe if I raised the calf to become a bull, I could some day coax Dan into starting his herd over again. The baby, fathered by Ferdinand, was the last of the Borges herd.

When Ron came in that evening, I showed him the calf and it sidled up to him.

"Well, Marn, what did you do this time? You know, if you raise this calf, it will be your full responsibility. I've already been dubbed the bad guy."

"I know. I've already bought suckle at the feed store. I named him Babe, after Paul Bunyan's blue ox."

We didn't see much of Dan Borges for some time. I think he had trouble controlling his emotions. A rumor circulated that he'd suffered a slight heart attack, and his wife Barbara actually felt relieved that he no longer worked in the cattle business.

I had fun showing the school children the calf. The baby grew and grew. Within a year, muscles developed around his barrel, and he grew a floppy loose fold of skin called a dewlap. Babe's head became a mass of dirty white curls with two protruding sharp nubs. I worried about his horns growing up instead of down. Then I remembered Dan's young bull calf wearing lead weights on his horns. They forced them to grow down like braces on a kid's teeth. I ordered a set from the feed store, and Ron helped me attach them. Within a year the restraints forced the horns downward, and they couldn't catch on barbed wire or hurt anything.

Babe soon grew into a strapping young teenager feeling his oats. His hooves looked as big around as the tree trunk of a two-year-old apple sapling. I kept him in the pasture on the hill, and each morning threw him a couple of flakes of alfalfa over the barbed wire fence. I think he anticipated my visits, because he would half run, half lumber over, not just for the food, but also for a head scratching. He closed his eyes and almost purred when I rubbed his forehead.

One day an interpreter, Gloria, set up a display

table under the trees, just up the hill a short distance from the barn. Babe was secure in the lower pasture. Gloria waited for the school children to arrive.

Suddenly, I heard a bellowing roar from the far fence. Standing square at the fence was our neighbor rancher's large Black Angus bull with an attraction for a couple of young heifers visiting the ranch for water.

Suddenly, I heard another familiar loud roar from the lower pasture. Before I could react, Babe crashed through the fence and headed full steam toward the other bull, mowing down every obstacle in his path.

He bowled down the interpreter's table, turning it on its side and scattering display items all over the hill. I could hear Gloria screaming, "You son of a gun!. . . Get out of here! You. . .!"

Worried that Babe had hurt Gloria, I grabbed Dan Borges' old bull crop off the wall in the barn. With the ease of a full-grown deer I leaped over the nearest barbed wire fence and stumbled up the hill. Gloria was picking up display items. "Are you all right?" I yelled.

"Yes, I think so, but I may need one of my glycerin pills. My heart's pounding a mile a minute. What in heaven's name was it that sailed over me? It just seemed to come out of thin air. Was that what I thought it was? A bull?"

"Yes, he was going after that other one up on

the hill above you," I gasped. "I've got to stop him before there's a fight and one of them gets hurt."

Gloria scanned the top of the hill near the trees. "I don't see any other bull," she said.

I looked up. The Black Angus had disappeared and Babe pawed the ground near the fence line, as if to say, "And I mean it. Stay away from my ranch. This is my territory."

When I neared Babe, he gently trotted down toward me. "You bad boy!" I screamed. "Darn you. You almost hurt somebody." I snapped the short bullwhip over his head, and for the first time he felt its sharp sting against his rump. I chased him into the large corral, where I slammed the gate shut behind him.

Another problem presented itself. Bully, as I now called him, needed a girlfriend. My animal fund contained some money, so I invested in a couple of young heifers.

A lady near Brentwood was selling her whole herd, and Ron and I drove there for a look. A Black Angus and a black and white bald face looked good. When I asked her the price, she said, "Make an offer."

"Fifty cents per pound?" I didn't know if it was a good or bad offer, but she nodded her head, saying, "I have to make a quick sale."

When the heifers arrived at the ranch, Bully took one look at the young ladies and without any instruction took over the duties of being a father.

About seven months later the bald face gave birth to a little red and white Hereford bull calf, the first of three calves Bully would sire.

After owning Bully for about four years, John Ginocchio, the new rancher, approached me. "Marnie, you know, you've got a fifties bull there."

"A what?" I said.

"A fifties bull. He's got horns. Most of the ranchers today want cattle that don't have horns. They even breed them so they don't grow horns. You should really get rid of him. I'd hate to see what'd happen if he got with my cows. I have enough problems as it is. Tell ya what. If you get rid of him, I'll let you breed your heifers with my bull. I'll even take him to auction for you."

I didn't want to sell Bully even if he was a fifties bull. I had raised him; he was my baby, and the last of the Borges herd. But it was a political situation I couldn't stop. On the day Bully clopped into the truck and headed for auction, my heart ached and tears rolled down my cheeks. Now I knew how Dan Borges must have felt when he parted with his cattle.

George Barber

A WET FEBRUARY provides ample grazing on the hill behind the Borges Ranch hay barn.

What a Hay Day

With the $1,800 we received for Bully, we purchased a two-year supply of alfalfa. On a hot September morning, about ten o'clock, a huge flatbed truck, stacked five tiers high and fourteen alfalfa bales long, parked in front of the windmill, its air brakes wheezing. The driver left the motor running while he hopped down from the cab. On his head he wore a red baseball cap with "Anderson's Trucking & Hauling, Lodi, California" stenciled in black across it. He wore soft leather tan workman's gloves and everyday cowboy boots that looked like they had walked through a few barnyards.

Ron greeted the trucker, who asked him where he wanted the hay unloaded. "Back your truck into the corral and unload it as close as possible, right in front of the barn, near the big open window," Ron said, then opened the large corral gate.

Skillfully, the driver first went forward for a short distance, then cautiously swung the tractor back around at an angle so it lined up perfectly with the barn; then he inched the truck backward, until he saw Ron's stop signal in his side view mirror.

Rich, Nancy and Dave from the maintenance crew and I stood by with hay hooks and gloves, ready to help unload.

The truck's hydraulic jacks operated a tilt bed that allowed the hay bales to partially slide off. Then with hay hooks and brute strength, we neatly positioned one layer of bales at a time, until they were all off the truck. It took more than an hour and a half, but it seemed a piece of cake compared with the daunting prospect of loading bales into the barn.

After signing the release form and watching the truck pull out, Ron left for an appointment, so it was up to the maintenance crew and me. We knew we faced a dirty, sweaty all-day job. At first we tried pushing, shoving and lifting the bales with our own sheer strength and the hay hooks, but it took forever and we were getting exhausted.

Rich and I stood sweating on the stack of bales outside the barn, while Nancy and Dave were in the barn. Rich said, "There must be a faster, better way of doing this. Anyone got any suggestions?"

Suddenly, a light bulb went on in my head. "I know!" I exclaimed, snapping my fingers.

"When Dan Borges loaded hay, he rigged up a block and tackle at the crest of the barn. He ran a long rope through it with a large hay hook attached at one end. He connected the other end to the front of his jeep parked in front of the barn at the back of the stack."

I described how he'd learned the technique from his father and grandfather, but back then they used his grandfather's huge French Percheron horses instead of a jeep. A helper standing on the stacks of bales would embed the hook in a bale of alfalfa, then signal the jeep driver to back up. As the truck moved backward with the rope, the other end of the rope with the hook moved forward toward the barn, dragging the bale of alfalfa with it. "It's a fairly simple technique, and I'm sure we can do it," I said.

A large old block and tackle and rope in the other barn could handle the job. In one of the interpretive displays, we found an antique hand-forged hook. It may not have been originally used for hay, but we figured it would work just fine for our purposes. We rigged up the block and tackle, then threaded the rope through, attaching the hook to one end and the other end of the rope to the bumper on Dave's work truck.

They made me the designated driver, since Rich had the strength to set the hook. After attaching the hook to the first bale, he gave the signal, and I slowly backed the truck as far as the rope extended; but it wasn't quite far enough to swing the bale forward all the way into the barn. Then Dave suggested attaching the rope to the winch on the truck. We could still back the truck up as far as the rope allowed, then use the winch as an extension, pulling it even farther. It worked, and with Rich's guidance, the bale swung easily into the barn in position on top of the other bales, where Dave and Nancy detached the hook and squared the bale with their hay hooks. They then swung the rope and hook back to Rich.

We experienced only one hang-up, when Nancy slipped on some slick old hay and one of her legs plunked down between the bales. "I'm all right," she insisted, but we all knew it must have hurt. The next day she said her tailbone ached and she was really stiff.

By late afternoon, the system operated smooth as silk. We'd loaded most of the bales when Ron showed up. "Wow!" he said. "I'm amazed at your ingenuity, and how much you accomplished in so little time."

The Heat Takes Its Toll

It was mid-July on a Saturday, when the temperature reached 106 degrees. Ranger Ron came in about 2 p.m., his hair damp and sweat drizzling down his face. His limp uniform shirt showed salt-ring stains under the arms. The dogs lay sprawled on the porch except when lapping the water from the bowls I filled several times that day.

Not a blade or leaf stirred. The stillness reminded me of the day the big earthquake rattled the countryside. Whiffs of heat rose from the ground like ghostly apparitions, and the air reeked of black sage and the licorice smell of fennel. On Sunday, Ron's day off, we escaped the heat by going across the bay for the day, hoping the three orphan calves on the hill behind the barn would find shade under the oak trees.

Early Monday morning Nancy, one of the maintenance workers, knocked on the door and caught me still in my bathrobe, just after stepping out of the shower. Ron had left at 4:30 a.m. to go fishing as usual.

Nancy looked concerned. "Staff brought the three Holstein calves down from the hill behind the barn this morning, and they're really sick. Can you come take a look?"

I told her, "As soon as I get dressed."

When I reached the barn, two of the calves were lying down and the third wobbled on splayed legs, slowly nibbling on a flake of alfalfa. All three calves were listless and their sides were gaunt. Gray matter oozed from their swollen, glazed eyes, and flies congregated on their backs and buzzed around their heads. I first thought they had somehow nibbled on the squirrel bait.

"I'm not sure what's making them sick," I said, "but I'll give John Ginocchio and Dan Borges, the ranchers, a call to see if they have any ideas."

Dan and John said it sounded like pink eye and suggested giving the calves shots of Tetramyacin. I hesitated because antibiotics sometimes stay in the meat a long time. Sensing my concern, John said, "I'll come over and take a look at them in about an hour. Hold off with the shots until I get there."

After John arrived, he checked the calves' eyes and said it didn't look like pink eye because there wasn't any redness around the eyes. He also wondered if they had eaten some squirrel bait. I asked Dave, one of the maintenance workers, if they had put any bait up on the hill and he said no. We finally concluded that heat stroke weakened the calves, preventing them from coming down to the water trough. As a result, they got severely dehydrated. Their eyes became irritated and infected from the numerous flies feeding on them.

John advised giving the calves some Gatorade diluted with water. Its high fructose or sugar water count would help until we bought electrolytes at the feed store. Electrolytes are full of nutrients, and react fast. "Buy Patriot fly ear tags, which repel flies," he added. The feed store stocked the electrolytes but no fly ear tags. I ordered the tags, and the clerk guaranteed me next day delivery by UPS.

The electrolytes helped, and for the next two days the calves appeared better. But on the third day, the weakest of the three calves came down with scours (bad diarrhea) and could barely stand. I gave it a large dose of Kaopectate, but that worked for only a short time. We kept a close watch over him most of the day, but that evening the calf, so weak it couldn't lift its head, was still squirting poop. Its entire body was feverish and moist, and its eyes had a glossy blank stare with a gray film over them, like an old dog blind with cataracts. I tried placing wet towels on its body, but it was too late. As I knelt by the calf, stroking its neck, its eyes rolled back in its head and its body went limp.

I felt a lump swell up in my throat. I had raised that calf with the other two since they were only a few days old. They licked my hand and followed me around like pet dogs. I even taught them how to drink from a nipple by dipping my thumb in the milk suckle and letting them suck on my thumb and fingers. Naturally, I had grown attached to them, so losing one proved heart wrenching. Worse yet, only a week before they frisked around the yard as we commented on how healthy they looked. I helped Ron drag the calf's carcass into the corral. He said he'd put it in a large trash bag and dispose of it. I then went into the house.

The next morning the maintenance staff shoveled the old bedding straw out of the barn and opened the doors and windows, letting in fresh air. They also put down new hay. We didn't want the dead calf's germs and feces contaminating the other two calves. We washed out the pails and nipples with hot soapy water, rinsed them thoroughly, and hung them on hooks where they could air dry.

On another feed store trip that day, I picked up the ear tag repellents and tag gun. That evening, Ron helped me give the calves their suckle. As they were busy sucking, I held the calves steady while Ron quickly squeezed the tag gun trigger, putting the red fly repellent tag through each one's ear. The gun was fast, like piercing a human ear. It must not have hurt much, because the calves only shook their heads slightly and continued with the business of sucking. The next morning, they looked much better. The flies no longer buzzed around them, and they wanted out in the back enclosure of the barn.

They continued growing stronger every day and within a month frolicked in the field again.

Trail Day

It was fall again and Trail Day. "Mornin', Ms. Marnie," yelled a volunteer from across the barnyard. "Goin' to help with the trails today?" I smiled and said I'd help with the barbecue but couldn't work on the trails, as I still had farm animals to feed. By 8:30 a.m. nearly forty people spread over the ranch, helping repair the damaged open space trails. It made me feel good and proud that people in the Walnut Creek community took pride in their trails and helped each fall. About twenty workers also showed up from the Esprit Clothing Outlet in San Francisco.

Ron, his new boss, Dan Cather, and two maintenance people organized the volunteers and gave them a brief talk about the city's open space program before loading them into vans and pickup trucks.

After the last van disappeared up the hill, I started my daily routine of feeding the farm animals. The sheep were bedded down on the ground, as if sensing a change in the weather. I placed several flakes of alfalfa in their feeder, and they slowly arose and ambled over to it. Usually they bowled me over in the rush for food. At the horse barn, Honey Bear already waited at her feeder under the shelter. When I said, "Mornin', Honey!" she flicked her head up and down, sniffed the air and snorted. She too sensed the pressure change.

A sudden chilly wind swirled the leaves and dust around my boots. A yellow-orange Baltimore oriole with shiny black hood and back gripped the fence rail and gently teetered back and forth in the breeze. I looked in vain for his pale mate. "Mornin', Yellow Bird," I said. "Looks like rain." He nodded an acknowledgment and skittered toward the almond tree.

As I crossed the corral to give the four black and white Holstein calves their morning ration of suckle and warm water, large dark pregnant clouds slid fast across the gray morning sky, dimming the faint sunlight. I shivered and hurried for the shelter of the cow barn.

As I closed the barn door, large raindrops started drumming a rhythmic tune on the tin roof. The calves, already inside, snuggled against each other for warmth, waiting patiently. I filled the five pails in the feed shed with warm water from the spigot and stirred in a cup and a half of powdered suckle mix in each. Then I brought the pails out and put them in the cutout holes in the milk bar. The calves pushed and shoved their way, rushing for the nipples, and it made me laugh and feel warm inside.

I thought of the volunteers, maintenance people, and rangers getting muddy and drenched in the cold rain. A few wore raincoats and boots in anticipation of a downpour, but the majority relied on just light jackets. I took a deep breath and smelled the rich aroma of fresh cowpies, trampled hay, and damp earth. The smell of wet earth reminded me of my grandma's vegetable garden in the early spring, when I was a little girl. I always loved that smell.

Again my thoughts focused on those who surely by now felt like "unhappy campers" out on the trails. I quickly washed out the calf pails, hung them on the hooks on the side of the barn, then scurried over to the other barn and covered picnic area. I had volunteered to start the coals in the barbecue about 11:30, but if the downpour continued I knew people would stagger in long before then.

The covered picnic area was a slippery, mucky river of mud, and several of the red and white checked tablecloths had blown off the picnic tables and lay crumpled against the fence. This would never do. Then an idea occurred: Build a fire in the stove in the recently restored horse barn, so the volunteers could at least warm themselves. On my way there, I stopped at the woodshed and gathered several armloads of the driest wood and brought it inside.

The rain continued its ratta-tat-tat dance on the tin roof, but it stayed nice and dry inside, because of the recent renovations. I made donuts out of rolled-up newspaper, put them in the stove, added kindling, and lit a match. First the paper, then the wood scraps burst into flame as I opened the flue and added small logs. Soon a warm fire gobbled up the chill. I spread the blown-off tablecloths over three tables in the barn and dried them with a rag.

The Walnut Creek Open Space Foundation members had provided only soft drinks for a beverage, which few people might choose on a cold rainy day. They needed something warm or hot like coffee or cocoa. In the cook shed I wrestled down two of the big coffee pots, filled them with water, and brought them into the barn. In one I made coffee and in the other I heated water. As I scrambled for paper cups, sugar and cream, I noticed two boxes of instant hot chocolate packets left over from the previous week's Environmental/Living History Program and decided that would be just the ticket along with the hot coffee.

About a half hour later the first of the volunteers tramped in, boots and tennis shoes mud-caked, hair plastered to their heads, shivering in dripping wet clothes. The rain poured as I instructed them to shed mud on the foot scraper before entering. I handed them towels, then ushered them into the barn, where I said, "Warm your backsides by the stove," and offered them coffee or cocoa. Smiles blossomed on cold wet faces. Soon the volunteers forgot the misery from the rain.

Gone Fishing

Many rangers work on Saturday or Sunday and take one or both of their days off during the week. Since we live where we work, we learned over the years that a trip is the only way we can truly relax without somebody bothering us. Ron says, "If I'm here [meaning the ranch], I'm working."

Some rangers enjoy hiking, western dancing, photography, bird watching, or riding motorcycles down the coast highway. Others, like my husband, like fishing.

So every chance that comes along, he goes fishing. Occasionally I'll go along as an escape or to keep him company. But being cramped in a small boat for eight hours with only a pickle bucket to pee in, getting seasick, and dealing with a crabby husband because the fish aren't biting is not my cup of tea. So, usually Ron heads out with one of his fishing buddies. I really don't mind, though, as it gives me a day alone for things that need doing, and unlike some women, I know where my husband is and what he is doing.

First hooked at the age of nine when an elderly man at a campground showed him how to bait a hook, Ron has caught salmon, bass, halibut, sturgeon, trout, Ling cod, Wahoo, red snapper, blue marlin, old rubber tires, license plates and crabs.

While in college, he took a fly-tying class from Walton Powell. Today he proudly wears a Fly Fishermen's Association member badge. Before we invested in a used Boston Whaler a few years back, Ron fished from piers, off the rocks, a party boat, or a small rented boat.

On every one of our vacations, fishing took at least one day, or it wasn't a vacation to Ron, and I couldn't live with him. Our trips include Baja, Mexico, along the entire coast of California, Oregon, Washington, Canada and Alaska, and recently the Florida Keys, where Ernest Hemingway wrote his famous book, *The Old Man and The Sea*.

I'll never forget one particular fishing adventure at Trinidad Bay in Northern California. Kim joined us, and we rented a small rowboat.

Ron strained mightily, drawing back the oars, aiming for the distant Split Rock. Meandering out of the harbor, he rowed through a maze of floating moorings, fishing boats and dinghies. We nearly grazed an old fishing boat. Her name, "Molly B.," was freshly painted in bold black letters across her white rusty hull. I said to myself, why bother?

Split Rock consists of two massive monoliths, barnacle and seaweed encrusted, protruding side by side out of the sea.

We found a floating mooring and tied up. Then

we waited, and we waited, and we waited.

Ron fumbled with the short-wave radio. It sent squawks and static into the sterile morning. We caught an old-time radio show of George Burns and Gracie Allen. We listened intently, charmed by their innocent banter.

The lamp from the old lighthouse blinked, its brilliant light projecting a red, green to gray image on the early morning sky.

Frothy tide water hiccuped against the sides of the boat. Its crawling effluvia crept into cracks and crevices over the leathery, green sea lettuce. Salt crystals resembling sugar-coated granules glistened with the clean morning sun.

Each surge of the tide bumped a tangled bulbous brown mass of kelp against the rocks. Tiny crabs scattered for shelter.

Then, without warning, an ominous silence alerted us. Where were the birds? The sea was as smooth as a grosgrain ribbon.

Large fish jumped, hoisting their entire bodies out of the water. From behind the rocks, we heard a soft lowly sound of two "Whooofffs" erupting from blow holes like steam escaping from an old radiator. The misty shower smelled like warm dead air from an old inner tube, mixed with the odor of rotting seaweed and plankton.

My heart leaped. Less than thirty feet away were a mother, over one hundred feet long, and her calf, their dark gray-blue backs mottled with

crinkly yellowish-white clusters of barnacles, their
bodies breaching, exposing giant flukes and tails.
"Gray whales!" we shouted.

George Barber

**JAKE AND SAM enjoy teasing now and then, but they
respond quickly to voice commands.**

It's a Daisy

After several weeks of torrential winter rains, the open space hills came alive again with warm spring sunshine and velvet green grass. Curly-leafed soap root, purple-blue Brodiaea called Ithuriel's Spear, and bright yellow buttercups splashed their neon paint upon the hills. Under the oaks fleshy clumps of Miner's lettuce awaited picking, and bright green buckeyes spread their welcome canopies.

One afternoon after closing the Visitor Center, I donned my hiking boots and grabbed the dogs' leashes. As I opened the front gate, the shepherd and black lab raced each other and waited for me at the back gate. They teased my slow form plodding up the hill behind them, trying my best to keep up, and every so often yelling, "Jake, Sam, wait up!" I didn't have to worry, though, because they were faithful dogs, rarely straying out of my sight, and upon voice command dashing back.

Near the new open space trail behind Twin Ponds was a small, swiftly running spring creek. While the dogs made their marks and sniffed out every rock and bush, I picked several tender leaves from some watercress plants rooted and floating in the creek. The peppery but mild taste left a slight tingling, refreshing feeling in my mouth.

I discovered several waterfalls created by spring runoff, and a treasure trove of wildflowers: blue forget-me-nots, Blue Dicks, pinkish-red shooting stars with black sharp tips, purplish-white pagoda-like Chinese Houses, white lacy Yarrow, and occasional bright showy yellow narrow-leafed Mule's Ear. A black-tailed deer and her spotted fawn daintily tiptoed up a hill. Blue jays darted across the ravine. The air carried a sweet earthy damp smell.

At the bridge, I listened and gazed at the rushing water spilling over smooth sandstone rocks and cascading aimlessly down the gully to the stream below. Fairy-like bracken ferns and small white flowers with yellow centers brightened an area beneath the bridge. I snapped a photo in my mind of what they looked like. "You must look the plant up in the plant book when you return," I vowed.

When I first married Ranger Ron, he was really enthused about the ethnobotany of plants and wanted me to share in his discoveries. Whenever we went hiking, he always asked if I could identify a particular flower or plant. It annoyed me—so much that I didn't enjoy our walks in the woods any more. One day, I thought I'd beat him at his game by identifying every new plant we found as a "daisy," even if it didn't resemble one. It really bugged Ron, but from then on he didn't drill me, and he let me enjoy nature in my own way. Identifying unknown plants as daisies now rates as a standard family joke.

The dogs drank some water as they investigated below the bridge; then we climbed the grassy slope. At Rocksprings, the dogs thought about exploring the pond, but danger lurked this early in the year. If one of them slipped and went in the water, an escape seemed unlikely. I didn't know if I could save him. He could drown like an Irish setter had at Bull Frog Pond when it was swollen with winter runoff, its banks pocked from the hooves of cattle, and its muddy banks black, gooey, slick muck. I called the dogs back, and we headed up the knoll toward the main fire road.

Brian Murphy

LOOKING somewhat like a German Shepherd, the coyote likes open fields and forests and brushy areas. Its diet consists of rodents and other small animals.

As we neared the trail, we spied a coyote. It didn't seem disturbed by our presence, but I attached the leashes to the dogs' collars, just in case.

The coyote stood frozen, watching a ground squirrel scurry out of its hole. It quickly pounced on its victim, which let out a shrill squeal, then was quiet. Turkey vultures circled overhead. The coyote picked up the squirrel, the plump limp body dangling from the corners of its mouth, and I spotted bright red blood oozing from the puncture wounds where the coyote had snapped the squirrel's neck with his teeth.

The coyote trotted along for some time, watching us from a safe distance. He didn't appear afraid of us, just curious. Suddenly he stopped, dropped the ground squirrel carcass, stared at me, then ripped the squirrel apart with his teeth. He quickly gulped down the large portions, barely chewing them. After his meal, he continued on a parallel path, still keeping his distance, but at a slower pace. Perhaps he was nearing his den.

As we reached the main trail, the coyote veered left up a wooded draw, stopped and stared at us again, as if studying us. The only motion he made was an occasional flick of his pointed wolf-like ears. His tawny, rust-spotted, scruffy coat blended perfectly with the scenery, and he was gone.

"Come on! Let's go home!" I shouted to the dogs. They pulled out, and we headed along the main Briones to Mt. Diablo Trail back to the ranch.

Borges Ranch Day

Dan's grandfather, Frank Borges, was born June 9, 1860. So each year on the Saturday closest to his birthday, the Borges Ranch Interpretive Association, Walnut Creek Open Space Foundation and City of Walnut Creek Open Space Division host Borges Ranch Day.

It's a one-day event lasting from 11 a.m. to 5 p.m. Entry is free. Families and individuals come from all over the East Bay to enjoy this special day.

For several weeks before the event, Ranger Ron, open space staff, volunteers, the interpreters and I work hard arranging for groups and individuals to entertain and help with the event. We distribute and post fliers and make up maps, schedules, menus, and directional signs. We order supplies and prepare special Portuguese food, arrange for the delivery of extra outhouses, and for shuttle buses that transport people from and back to the parking lot at Northgate High School.

In past years we've enjoyed "Foggy Mountain Jam," a bluegrass band, plus country and western live bands, but this year—1994—as our highlight, we hired authentic Portuguese dancers, who whirled in front of the barn to the music of the Azores in their colorful red, black, white and gold embroidered costumes.

As the shuttle lets people off near the blacksmith shop, they first meet Jerry Bishop, a skilled blacksmith and long-time interpreter at the ranch. Jerry first came as a ranch visitor one day, a recent retiree from the Castro Valley School District after teaching thirty years. Ron was showing him the blacksmith shop when a large group of school children arrived and gathered around Jerry and Ron. The phone rang, and Ron ran for it, leaving Jerry with the kids. Jerry repeated what Ron had just told him about the anvil and the forge, and showed them around. From then on he was hooked and ever since has demonstrated his skills as a blacksmith at the Borges Ranch.

At the old-fashioned windmill you can pump water from an eighty-foot well. We only ask that you please water a tree or plant with it.

Near the wagon shed and around the corner across from the woodpile, the Early Day Gas Engine and Tractor Association set up a marvelous display of working machinery. The corn grinders, pencil sharpeners, apple corers, water pumps, and choppers clank, wheeze and emit a puckata, puckata, fissta chorus.

In the restored Borges barn your child can have his or her face painted or make an Indian bead bracelet while you visit the country store for a jar of delicious strawberry jam made on the ranch. At another table, volunteers sell food tickets for hamburgers, hot dogs, Portuguese sopas, beans, and donuts.

At the small animal corral, 4-H kids show you how they shear their sheep. You can also visit the other farm animals, such as the horse, pigs, goats, chickens and rabbits.

Then venture into the old house and Visitor Center where the National Charity League volunteers take you on a special tour. In the old-time kitchen there is a 1903 Stewart cast-iron stove, freestanding kitchen cabinets, a multitude of fascinating labor-saving devices, and a crank telephone on the wall. Put its receiver on your ear and eavesdrop on some 1906 gossip.

The bathroom by the kitchen sports a tin tub, and on the opposite side, the pantry includes a rocker washer and cream separator. In the parlor down the hall, some wonderful displays depict the turn of the century, such as entertainment, inventions, and Borges family memorabilia. Sitting at her spinning wheel you may find Wilma Seppala, also a retired school teacher and lover of the arts. Wilma can tell you how wool and other fibers are spun or woven into cloth and yarn for sweaters.

As you leave, peek in the bedroom with its 1910 brass bed, thunder mug, clothing, commode, and children's toys.

Then head down the front stairs. At the picnic

tables you will meet other interpreters and volunteers who show your children how to tool leather and make rope and cornhusk dolls. On the grass a crowd of people may be watching their children bat a candy-filled piñata.

End your day with a tall glass of homemade lemonade or a slice of watermelon, and it's likely you'll hanker to come back next year.

The Walnut Creek Open Space also hosts its annual Borges Ranch "Holiday Hoedown" the first weekend in December, a Harvest Festival in October at the Howe Homestead Park, and a Halloween Celebration at the Sugarloaf Ranger Station.

George Barber

EXCELLENT CARE by 4-H Club members produces award-winning animals like this goat.

Awards Banquet

Each year the City of Walnut Creek holds its annual awards banquet, honoring city employees who have reached five, ten, fifteen, twenty, twenty-five and thirty years. The city also presents two Employee of the Year Awards then. No one knows who will receive these awards. If possible, Ron and I attend the banquet every year, even if Ron isn't up for an award, just to support his co-workers.

The 1994 banquet took place at the prestigious Boundary Oaks Golf Course Savoy Restaurant. Ron, who prefers casual dress, obliged me by donning his one special-occasion suit, and wore a tie with the image of a fisherman on it. Kim gave him the tie as a gag gift the year before for Christmas. I wore a simple pink, gold and black paisley dinner dress I bought for our twenty-second wedding anniversary.

The scrumptious and filling dinner featured large overstuffed breasts of chicken called Fountain Blue, after a restaurant in New Orleans that introduced the dish. I couldn't eat it all, so Ron motioned for me to transfer what remained onto his plate. For dessert the waiter brought Ron's favorite cheesecake with raspberry sauce.

After the dinner, City Manager Don Blubaugh started giving out the awards along with several other members of the executive team. After the final thirty-year award, the city manager set the stage for the Employee of the Year Award.

Forty employees, including Ron, had been nominated. We thought Ron made the list as a nominee because of winning an Extra-Mile Award previously in the year. He'd transported an ice cream cart and ice cream to the city picnic, which seemed a pretty easy way of earning a "Blue Buck." If an employee receives an Extra-Mile Award during the year, his or her name automatically goes on the list.

When the city manager said the City of Walnut Creek hired the employee seventeen years ago and he had worked as a ranger at the Petrified Forest National Park in Arizona, Ron's ears perked up. He then knew who the city manager was describing and that he was one of the honorees. When Don Blubaugh called Ron forward to receive the award, my heart leaped and I could feel my legs nervously twitch underneath the table.

I proudly watched Ron strut up to the podium. He then turned and whispered something in the manager's ear. "You're way ahead of me, Ron," he said. "Marnie, will you come up also?" Even though the Employee of the Year Award is only for city employees, I knew Ron had said he wanted to share his award with me.

I smiled at Ron and found myself striding toward the podium and my rightful place alongside my husband. I nervously wondered how I looked standing next to him. My hands and arms felt awkward, and hung loosely at my sides. I thanked my lucky stars I'd worn my nicest dress. City Manager Blubaugh presented Ron with a beautiful wooden and bronze plaque engraved with the city's oak tree logo, Ron's name, the year 1994, and the words Employee of the Year. The manager shook our hands and a photographer snapped our picture standing next to each other. The city manager asked if we wanted to say a few words.

Ron said something like, "We're not just husband and wife, but a team." He added, "It just isn't my wife and I who worked in the open space, but also many people in our community who helped over the years." When my turn came, I said modestly, "I have worked in many offices in this city, but my heart is in the open space." The entire room applauded. At this point I retreated to my seat.

The other Employee of the Year Award went to Debbie Fudala, Reprographics Department supervisor. Her husband Rich had just started as a maintenance worker with open space. Debbie and Ron were asked to pull the winning tickets for the door prizes. The first names Ron pulled out of the hat were Ron and Marnie White. Embarrassed, he put the ticket back and chose another.

After the banquet, many people congratulated us. Ron beamed as he shook people's hands. It felt really good knowing my husband was worthy of such an honor, and that he considered me a part of his team.

Ron turned to me, smiled and said, "I want you to know, this plaque is half yours."

George Barber

RANGER RON WHITE stands behind the sign that welcomes visitors to the Walnut Creek, California, ranch.

But Then Came Fall
By Marnie White

I remember the knothole in the outhouse door
you stuffed with a scrap of burlap sack
the gray shroud of dusty cobwebs
flapping like an old dishcloth
in the dry wind

I remember the dark splatter of blackbirds
circling over the crest of the barn
how they would sometimes make you shudder
their fixed yellow eyes staring
always staring

I remember the creak of the windmill
slowly turning in the hot sun
and the sweet mossy taste of cool water
in your cup from the pump

But then came fall
the ants ceased their endless trail
leading from the molasses block to a crack
in the floor boards of the barn
do you remember how we watched them
as if nothing else mattered

But then only yesterday
the scarecrow in the garden stood proud
his tattered hat tied on
with a piece of twine
the bright yellow sunflowers withered

leaning against him for support
and then, there was the old walnut tree
rope swing dangling from its lowest branch
heavy with this year's crop

the dark-brown stain from its hulls
permanently etched upon our palms
But then towards evening once again
came the lowly cry for the weaned calf

* * * * *

"*But Then Came Fall*" won second place in the 1985-86 Robert Browning Society Awards. This poem was written when my oldest daughter left home for college.

George Barber

"I REMEMBER the creak of the windmill slowly turning in the hot sun. . .the sweet mossy taste of cool water. . ."